Step Aside for Royalty

Step Aside for Royalty

Treasured Memories of the Royal Household

by
Eileen Parker

Step Aside for Royalty
By Eileen Parker

Cover design by Lucy Llewellyn at Head & Heart
Typesetting by Aimee Dewar at Head & Heart

Contents

Introduction

This little gem of a Buckingham Palace memoir was first published in 1982. Extracts were serialised in the *News of the World* to coincide with the wedding of Prince Charles and Lady Diana Spencer, but not because Eileen Parker had scandal to report. It could never have been that kind of book because Eileen was not that kind of person. Having been on terms of friendly familiarity with the Queen and Prince Philip for years she knew where her loyalties lay – 'I am a royalist. So no seedy revelations!'

The aim was to transcribe Eileen's experience into an authentic, first person account of life at Court in the first decade of the Queen's reign, the good times and the not so good. Public libraries were keen but the initial print run for *Step Aside For Royalty* was a meagre 1,500 copies and the promised paperback edition never appeared. As far as

Royalty was concerned, Princess Diana had changed the rules of the game. The world watched transfixed as that shy English rose blossomed first into the loving mother of princes and then into a bewitching international celebrity.

The book that Eileen and I wrote together missed its moment, but it went on to provide rich pickings for other writers. It cannot be easy to construct a book-length story about people one has only seen from a distance and whose inscrutability is so well defended. Eileen, with her wealth of inside knowledge, felt almost sympathetic – 'Most of them have never even met the Royal Family. I know what I'm talking about. I was there. I was part of it.'

Our publisher mangled the original text with stylistic intrusions that left us both feeling embarrassed. In this second edition I have tried to rescue Eileen's tone of voice. That's how *Step Aside For Royalty* took shape, as a series of transcribed conversations at the kitchen table in Eileen's country cottage. The flow of the narrative, to and fro, reflects the way her memories first arrived on the page, as spoken reminiscence. Reading her book today is like having her in the room once more, walking the walk, talking the talk. She was there. Eileen was part of it. In this book, she's living it still.

Chris Moore, London, November 2017.

Chapter 1

The Glitter and the Gold

London, England. Monday, 17ᵗʰ November 1947. 7.30 p.m.

Gliding up the wide avenue of the royal Mall, Mike and I peered out of our hired limousine to wave back at the swarming crowd cheering our progress. Above the revelry, framed by the Mall's leafless trees, the austere grandeur of Buckingham Palace stood stark in a blaze of floodlights. All of London was being drawn in the same direction. The heir to the throne, Princess Elizabeth, was getting married to Mike's closest war-time friend – Philip, Prince of Greece. Inside the palace, under the sparkling chandeliers, sipping champagne, the family of cousins representing the crowned heads of Europe was gathering for its biggest celebration since the downfall of Nazi Germany. England's bombed-out capital was determined to share in the cheerfulness.

As our cavalcade of cars was waved through the palace gates, a woman in the crowd pointed at us – 'Look, an admiral and his wife!'

Mike did indeed cut a dashing figure with all his medals on display, but he was actually wearing the dress uniform of a lowly Lieutenant of the Royal Navy. Typically, he turned it into a joke by playing the part and waving back with a smile. But it wasn't a joke. In ten minutes' time we really were going to be mingling with kings and queens. Was my hair all right? My ball-gown? It was an off-the-shoulder design in white satin from a Glasgow department store. I wore it with a single strand of pearls and my mother's fur coat. The effect I had been aiming for was the only one possible at a time of strict post-war rationing – neat and simple. But perhaps I was looking too neat, too simple?

The car drew up under a porch. A footman in State Livery came forward. Mike sensed my nervousness and with a soft word squeezed my arm reassuringly. I adjusted the corsage of flowers at my shoulder and stepped for the first time onto the red carpet of Buckingham Palace.

Footmen in scarlet tails and powdered wigs ushered us inside. We left our coats and took our place in the queue waiting to be presented to the Royal Family, gazing round at the splendour of the room with its gilt decoration and handsome furniture. My own war-time wedding, the only similar event I had for comparison, had been attended by a mere twenty guests with a guard of honour consisting of naval officers and fellow recruits serving in the Women's Royal Naval Service, WRNS, the Wrens. My experience of parties had been noisy affairs in the cramped quarters of a naval wardroom. The busy life of a Wren on a succession of Scottish naval bases had broadened my social outlook and made me better at handling my shyness, but how was one to supposed to cope with a glittering reunion of royalty?

It felt slightly reassuring to see so many of the men still in military uniform. One of them came over to talk, Lt.-Commander Peter Ashmore, an equerry to King George VI, the father of the bride-to-be. Mike had met Peter as part of the process of being appointed to the Royal Household as Prince Philip's equerry. He greeted us warmly and smiled as he spied the corsage of three carnations I was wearing – 'I can see nobody else here,' he murmured, 'wearing such an interesting decoration.'

I took a quick look round. Not one of the other women was wearing flowers, only jewels. I made an excuse and sidled over to a tall standing vase, and by the time our names were called out I had had made the necessary adjustment. Taking a deep breath I started walking towards the Royal Family – His Majesty, Queen Elizabeth, their daughter, Princess Elizabeth, and her fiancé, Prince Philip. Mike had coached me on the correct way to curtsey and how to hold out my hand, limply, with the palm inwards, for the single squeeze of the royal handshake – 'Whatever happens, don't squeeze back.'

Mike had also warned me about the King's stammer. In the unlikely event of His Majesty actually talking to me, I was not to prompt him if he ran into difficulties. Nor to speak at all unless spoken to first.

The King was shorter than I had anticipated, not much taller than my own five foot three inches. His face was notable for its high cheekbones but there were strong lines of anxiety around his blue eyes. As we were presented, His Majesty remained silent, but when we passed the Queen I heard her remark to Mike – 'What a lovely wee wife you have got!' I felt grateful for that – Her Majesty letting me know that she understood the calming effect of a compliment. It was part of Queen Elizabeth's charm to put people at ease.

Prince Philip was as handsome and debonair as I remembered him. We hadn't met since our Royal Navy days in Scotland during the war and he welcomed me now more as an old wartime acquaintance than the wife of his first-ever equerry.

The presentations continued until the last guest had been welcomed, by which time a circle had formed around the Music Room. At a pre-arranged signal, the Carroll Gibbons band, packed with rhythm and brass, launched into an up-tempo medley from the stage musical *Oklahoma*. Princess Elizabeth's Private Secretary, John 'Jock' Colville, turned to Mike – 'The Navy's got to start off the dancing.'

He meant us! And Jock Colville was not someone to ignore. The son of a former courtier himself, he had been one of Sir Winston Churchill's private secretaries during the war. I felt my arms and legs fail me. Mike, however, firmly but gently took me in hand again, and steered me onto the empty dance floor. Away we went, instinctively in step with the music, just as we had danced so many times before. Luckily, it was a foxtrot, one of my favourites.

After a couple of circuits, when everyone else had joined in, we felt able to relax slightly and take in the glittering array. The King, in tails, sailed by with his lovely Queen, who wore the blue sash of the Order of the Garter across her white evening gown, embroidered with silver and pearls. The Duchess of Kent partnered the King of Norway. The bride's sister and teenage bridesmaid, Princess Margaret, whirled past in the arms of a handsome Guards officer. Princess Elizabeth, in a creation of coral net, chatted gaily with her fiancé. Then I saw Lord Louis Mountbatten with his wife Edwina in his arms. Lord Louis was Prince Philip's uncle and his prime mentor in England but all I could think of was the last time I had seen him, in entirely different circumstances – at a damp and dreary dockyard with me wearing the thick, blue serge and peaked cap of my naval uniform and him inspecting the guard. I was entering a whole new world.

As the evening continued, I tried to identify more faces on the guest-list. I recognised Princess Juliana of Holland in conversation with, I think, the Queen of Greece, while Queen Ena of Spain, stunning in black and a dazzle of diamonds, appeared to be asking a question of Lady Mary Strachey, distinguished by the diamond 'E' pinned to her dress that identified her as one of the Ladies-in-Waiting to Princess Elizabeth. Someone remarked to me, surveying the living tapestry, that we must be witnessing one of the largest gatherings of Europe's royal families that had ever taken place. During the course of the evening more and more royal personages were pointed out, including King Frederik and Queen Ingrid of Denmark, the King and Queen of Yugoslavia, King Faisal of Iraq, Queen Helen of Rumania, the Prince Regent of Belgium and the Crown Prince and Princess of Sweden.

Mike provided me with a running commentary on the famous military and political figures, many of whom I recognised. I spotted Lord Halifax, a rather gaunt, very tall politician who also stood out because of his false left hand, which he wore in a glove. During a pause in the dancing Prince Philip brought over two other politicians – the Marquis of Salisbury and Lord Tweedsmuir, better known as John Buchan, the novelist and writer of thrillers like *Greenmantle* and *The Thirty-Nine Steps*. The former was one of the King's favourite shooting partners, known in the Household as Bobbety Cranbourne and famously easy to mimic because he pronounced his r as a w – as in wabbit and Wobert. While Bobbety engaged Mike in conversation I chatted with Lord Tweedsmuir about those parts of Scotland we knew in common.

The banquet was served in the State Dining Room. Each table was set for eight guests, with five footmen to wait on them. For the first time in my life I dined off gold plate – lobster mayonnaise, turkey with vegetables, vanilla soufflé and cherries in brandy. As well as champagne, and perhaps bearing in mind more military tastes, a bottle of Worthington's beer had been placed by each setting. The centrepiece of each table was a gold vase of pale yellow roses, white carnations and tropical foliage. The great room hummed with the convivial sound of conversation and laughter while the servants busied themselves among the lustre of jewels and medals.

After the banquet, the dancing resumed in a more relaxed party atmosphere. Prince Philip called for one of the Royal Navy's traditional war-time exuberances, the Hokey-Cokey, which I noticed Princess Margaret enjoying enormously, followed by the Palais Glide and then the Conga. Princess Elizabeth led the line of dancers out of the Music Room, threaded them through the Picture Gallery, back into the Blue Drawing Room, and then round again, back to the beginning, at which point the King and Queen joined in. I distinctly heard her whisper – 'I mustn't miss this, Bertie.' She held her robe with one hand and clutched the King's coat-tails with the other. Behind them was the Duchess of Kent, similarly attached to King Haakon of Norway. The Mountbattens, with Lady Edwina in a superb white gown and diamonds, provided the sting in the tail.

At about four o'clock in the morning, while the King was having a quiet smoke in a corner, I noticed him give a slight nod of his head. Carroll Gibbons smoothly brought his orchestra into the very last dance, and the King and Queen took the floor for a slow waltz. Then, after standing to attention for the national anthem, Princess Elizabeth and Prince Philip bade their guests goodnight.

Mike and I arrived back at our hotel with a huge sense of relief at having coped successfully with such a remarkable evening. Lingering over a last nightcap, our heads still buzzing, I wondered how much more of such 'duty' I could expect to come my way – and where it might lead if Mike stayed with Prince Philip?

'Who knows?' he said. 'I might be made the Governor of a far-off island in the sun … or something.'

* * *

Tuesday, 18th November, 9 p.m.

Tonight's wedding party was an even bigger event, attended not just by the Royal Family and their cousins but by all the great men of the realm – generals and admirals, politicians and judges, the leading figures of the day and their wives. Everybody who was anybody in the British Establishment was present, including the Labour Party's standard-bearer for the working man, Aneurin Bevan, the Minister for

Health, who stood out conspicuously as the only man in a lounge suit.

Instead of a banquet, a buffet supper was laid out on trestle tables – caviare, vol-au-vents, chocolate gateau – while the servants circulated with champagne. Last night's ball, grand as it was, had been a comparatively intimate and informal affair, with a preponderance of friends and family. At tonight's event, everybody was very much on his or her best behaviour.

Mike and I were standing with some of his fellow officers from the Pacific Fleet, when Prince Philip approached to introduce his fiancée, Princess Elizabeth. I remembered my curtsey but what on earth was I going to say? As soon as the Princess spoke, she put us at ease.

'Philip has told me all about you,' she said. 'Where are you all now?'

We chatted away for a while and then Prince Philip went off to fetch someone else – Queen Mary, the bride-to-be's grandmother. At eighty years old, intensely aware of her regal birthright, she could be a somewhat overpowering personality. I remember her opening remark to Commander Norfolk – 'Was he a good boy, then?' she asked him, with an inclination of her tiara in the direction of Prince Philip.

George Norfolk, who had been Prince Philip's captain in the destroyer *H.M.S. Whelp*, gave the only possible tactful reply. With a twinkle, Queen Mary pronounced herself convinced before allowing Prince Philip to move her on.

By now, having had so much practise the night before, I was more confident of how to handle myself and gave Her Majesty a perfect low curtsey when her eyes met mine, and that was enough.

Before Prince Philip left to attend to the rest of his guests he produced another surprise – 'There's just one more person I think you ought to meet.'

Walking across the room he returned with Sir Winston Churchill. The great man grunted an acknowledgement, leant back with his hands on his hips and beamed benevolently – 'Isn't this a marvellous occasion?' he exclaimed, with a sweep of his arm. 'Isn't this a simply *marvellous* occasion?'

He was clearly loving every minute. Whatever misgivings Sir Winston might have had prior to Princess Elizabeth's engagement to her foreign Prince, his amiable manner suggested he had been completely won over. Prince Philip handled him with a well balanced mixture of humour and respect – 'I suppose,' he mused, indicating the wives and men present, 'we had better preserve some decorum. You'd better shake hands with her first, sir. Her husband's a Commander ...'

I, of course, as the appendage of the newest and most junior equerry in the Household, was last in the order of seniority.

After the buffet, we danced again, this time in the crimson-walled Ballroom with a band of Guardsmen playing in the gallery. Before the War, the room had been used to hold the Royal Court; at one end were the thrones used by the King and Queen, surrounded, floor to ceiling by chrysanthemums and whatever blooms had survived from the previous evening. The war-time habit of recycling had become ingrained. We had become a thrifty nation. Soap was rationed, as was tea and sugar, almost everything. And if something wasn't rationed that was usually because it was unobtainable, except to those in the know. Sir Winston Churchill was still able, somehow, to keep himself in Havana cigars but the rest of us had to 'make do and mend' – or do without.

Again the music consisted mainly of selections from the hit musicals of the day, *Oklahoma* and *Annie Get Your Gun*. The favourite melody of the evening was *People Will Say We're In Love* which was reputed to be Princess Elizabeth's particular choice. In between dances Mike and I continued our exploration of the Palace corridors that we had begun the previous evening.

In general, Buckingham Palace seemed to have escaped really serious long-term damage. Although the chapel had been destroyed, the main State Rooms and the personal apartments of the Royal Family remained intact. But in the Picture Gallery, for instance, I noticed that the brocade upholstery was worn right through in places and nearly all the seats were threadbare.

With later familiarity I grew to recognise the obvious difference between the public rooms of the Palace and the private suites where the Royal Family lived. At the time, however, the building had a somewhat tired and gloomy ambience, a cross between a large provincial hotel and an unvisited, rather murky museum. The corridors were long and dark, their walls stained by a succession of damp London smogs. The floorboards creaked. The books in the bookcases gave the appearance of never having been read. The style throughout was solid and ponderous. In the ladies' cloakroom, for example, there was an abundance of marble and mahogany. The brass fittings were scrupulously bright, gleaming from years and years of painstaking polishing.

In the years that Mike worked for Prince Philip, first at Clarence House then at Buckingham Palace, I can only recall going 'below stairs' once, on the evening of the King and Queen's silver wedding anniversary in 1948. That morning, the Household had attended a Thanksgiving Service in St. Paul's, but as a more personal gesture the Royal couple arranged a cocktail party for the evening. We stood inside the tall french doors, sipping our drinks while watching the crowd surge to and fro behind the Palace railings. People were shouting (and singing) for a balcony appearance and their demands were growing louder.

Prince Philip warned Mike that nobody would be able to get in or out of the Palace until the early hours of the morning but that was no good for me – I had assured our baby-sitter that I wouldn't be late. Mike's solution was to sneak me out the back way, through the Royal Mews. But before we could get anywhere near the stables we had to go down into the basement, an absolute labyrinth of twists and turns more like an underground village than the cellars of a single building.

The Royal Household and staff number hundreds of people. Buckingham Palace is not only the London home of the reigning monarch but the administrative centre of 'the Crown'. By far, the majority of the six hundred rooms are offices. Buckingham Palace even has its own Post Office. The private apartments are located on the corner of the first floor overlooking Constitution Hill, separated from the 'business' corridors by doors covered with green baize. Behind these doors the Royal Family live their private lives, but everywhere else in the Palace they are on duty. It could almost be compared to lodging in a block of offices.

Eventually, Mike and I found our way through the maze of corridors, one of which, if I recall correctly, ran the entire length of the Palace. Outside, we found the one car that was always parked outside the Privy Purse door. It set me thinking, on the way home, about this strange new life we were leading – to realise that at the precise moment when thousands of people outside the palace would have been thrilled to get *in*, we had been frantically trying to get *out*.

* * *

Chapter 2

Philip, Prince of Greece

My father, Alexander Robert Allan, was a successful manufacturer of steel ropes in the Glasgow shipbuilding industry. He had joined his father's firm – Allan, Whyte – as an apprentice and risen to managing director. Our family home was in the small town of Troon on the Ayrshire coast, well away from the grime and smoke of the shipyards. Every weekday morning, Kelly, the chauffeur, would drive my father to the train station and in the evening make the same journey to bring him back home. What happened in between was a mystery to me. I can recall visiting the factory only once, when I was about eleven years old, when the launch cable for the giant liner *Queen Mary* was being made. My father informed me proudly that it was one of the largest ropes ever seen on the Clyde or anywhere else.

At an early age I was sent away to school because my

parents believed that an only child could easily become a lonely child. In the days before the Second World War, Troon was still a resort town. For a short summer season every year, Troon would be busy with holidaymakers and trippers. The rest of the time it was a placid backwater.

I did not like playing with dolls nor did I ever relish being told what to do. I was the typical tomboy. If a group of us were climbing trees, I wanted to be furthest off the ground. Whatever my playmates wanted to do, I would suggest something more daring. My poor dear mother often found herself caught between annoyance and bewilderment at this headstrong creature she had brought into the world.

Like most children of my background, when the time came for my proper education to begin, I was packed off to boarding school. The one I remember best was called Calder Girls' School, a bleak place on a wind-swept stretch of the Cumberland coast. The curriculum included lots of bracing lacrosse, and the discipline was rigid. Tuck was not allowed but had to be smuggled in and kept hidden at the start of every term.

The staff, commanded by an austere headmistress, Miss Bellamy, prepared round pegs for society's round holes with practised skill. She was our maths teacher as well as headmistress. Once, she gave me two marks out of a hundred in an arithmetic test. I loathed Maths, loved History, Biology and Games. But I was not a good scholar, nor was I always obedient.

Apart from the occasional trips into Glasgow for new school uniforms, my holidays, for as long as I can remember, were devoted to sport. Our house in Troon, called *Windygates*, was sandwiched between two golf courses. From the age when I could hold myself upright in a headwind, I used to waddle after my father with a fistful of shortened golf clubs. I had a pony to ride and was brought up to love fishing, but golf was my passion. My father was devoted to the game and played it all year round. Following his relentless enthusiasm, I became a proficient amateur and as I grew I started to collect prizes.

My father treated me with Victorian strictness, for he had been brought up to expect nothing better from life than the rewards he could win by hard work and thrift. My mother was more sympathetic, perhaps because she was the only girl in a family of five brothers. All she wanted after her marriage was to be cared for and protected in the style to which she had become accustomed. Father saw it as his privilege to oblige. While he worked at spinning his ropes and hawsers, my mother entertained her friends to luncheon and tea and ran the home.

The outbreak of the Second World War in 1939 changed everything. After the first heavy bombing of Glasgow by the Germans, certain Scottish towns, including Troon, were designated as safe areas and used as evacuation zones. In due course, an official arrived at *Windygates* to assess it. Our house had six bedrooms as well as quarters for the three live-in servants, but what excited the official more than anything were the four bathrooms. *Four* bathrooms! That scored lots of points.

Within a week our home was invaded by half a dozen evacuee women and children. My father shrugged his shoulders. It was the war; what could he do? We were lucky to have a roof over our heads, let alone bathrooms to spare. My mother was paid a little inconvenience money and supervised all the ration books. Otherwise, she settled into a state of siege in her own home. Her uninvited guests, unused to central heating, developed continuous colds and the younger ones wiped their noses on whatever happened to be to hand, sometimes the curtains or the carpet.

For me, the newcomers provided a change of routine. For my father, they were a mere nuisance. But the arrival of the evacuees fell on my mother as a calamity. The maid and the cook implored her to restore order in the home now reduced to chaos. It came as a relief when the Royal Navy came to the rescue by requisitioning *Windygates* for use as a Wren Officers' Mess. From this point on, my parents lived in a succession of hotels and rented houses until the war was over. When they did return, it was difficult to resume where they had left off. The reliable Kelly had been one of the early casualties to the call-up and, as the war bit deep into the nation's manpower, cooks, maids and other domestics found more essential and better paid jobs. There was plenty of war-work around Troon to occupy willing hands.

Today, many of Troon's larger houses, including *Windygates*, have been partitioned into flats. Whenever I return, I always drive past my old front door. The roses my father planted with my help still flower, but nothing else of my childhood remains.

* * *

As soon as war was declared I was eager to join up, but it wasn't until the Battle of Britain in the summer of 1940 that the staff of Calder Girls School closed their doors on me for the last time. I was glad to be free. The war, at that early stage, was exciting. On my return to Troon, I immediately volunteered for the first war-work I could find – in the British Legion canteen, brewing tea and frying eggs.

I had not been naïve enough to think I would be parachuted behind enemy lines on vital clandestine assignments, but I hadn't expected to be stuck in a scullery. One by one my Troon friends were disappearing amid vague rumours that they had lied about their ages to join up. I learned later that some of them never made it further than the local munitions factory but, at the time, I felt desperately anxious that I was in danger of missing the war altogether.

One day, instead of clocking on at the canteen, I caught the train to Glasgow and headed for *H.M.S. Scotia*, otherwise known as St. Enoch's Hotel. It was an overcast winter's day, grey and depressing. Blustery squalls of wind swept along the gutters and everybody seemed too preoccupied to give me coherent directions. I began to doubt my little scheme so much that, when I did find the place and was asked about my age, I nearly told the truth.

For some reason the Women's Royal Naval Service, the Wrens, had seemed a natural choice, but when asked what category of work I would prefer, I had to think fast. I could not type. I did not know shorthand. I had no secretarial qualifications of any kind. No, I hadn't worked a telephone switchboard. No, I could not cook. And as far as ships and boats were concerned, and despite my father running one of the country's biggest rope factories, I had only been to sea two or three times in my life.

That's when I announced that I could drive a car, which was true, up to a point. My father had not been too pleased when I asked him for driving lessons, and during the few times he took me out he quickly lost patience. Kelly, our chauffeur, had had to take over and thanks to his calm tutelage I did at least know the difference between the brake and the accelerator.

An examiner took me into the courtyard where an old Vauxhall was waiting. She got in the passenger seat beside me and pointed at the gate – 'Get in and out of there in one piece and you're good enough for us,' she said. Which I did. Having arrived as a schoolgirl I went home as a Wren. What joy!

I was told it would be some weeks before I could be inducted into uniform. In the interim I was given a W.R.N.S.

armband to wear on my sleeve. My father was aghast but in the arguments that followed Mother took my side and eventually he calmed down, especially when I explained that, in view of my age, I was almost certain to get an 'immobile' posting. Troon was a base for re-fitting submarines so in all probability I wouldn't even have to leave home.

The first two months of training were spent ten miles away at a place called Ardrossan, probably one of the least favourite dockyards in the Royal Navy, for it was gloomy, dank and dirty. I had to get up for work at five-thirty and spent my days learning about the internal combustion engine. As a driver I also had to acquaint myself with the layout of the naval and military bases I might have to visit. All this time I stayed quite near home with my paternal grandparents and came back in the evenings to their blissfully peaceful home, where the entertainment consisted of embroidery or listening to the BBC on the radio, which every night brought more news of Adolf Hitler's seemingly unstoppable conquests.

By the time I was drafted back to Troon, I had begun to realise along with everyone else that the war against Hitler was going to be a long one. Still, there were compensations. Only recently released from the constrictions of an English boarding school, I wasted no time in catching up with my more sophisticated colleagues. Wrens were a scarce commodity in Troon and there was always a flotilla of young officers queuing up for escort duty. The centre of our social life was the Marine Hotel, situated conveniently only a two-minute stroll along South Beach from *Windygates*. War-time restrictions and shortages had dulled some of the hotel's shine, but it was still the main venue for a dance or party. Most evenings of the week, the three Walker sisters and I would be there, flirting with a quartet of polished young beaux. Otherwise, there might be a film with the Marx Brothers or Bob Hope at the local cinema, followed by a preview of the latest record by the Ink Spots in someone's cramped attic lodging. It was an exciting time for a young girl who was no sooner in uniform than in love.

His name was Dal Russel, the Dal being short for Dalziel. He went on to become one of the most decorated of Canada's Second World War aviation heroes, but I first knew him as an ordinary fighter pilot – tall, blond and stunningly good looking. My parents seemed to like him too, despite the usual reservations from my father. Dal and I saw as much of each other as possible until his return to Canada for re-training. Afterwards, we attempted to exchange letters but he was a poor correspondent and I was no better. Some parcels of 'candy' arrived but it was war-time and as one of Troon's prize Wrens I was not short of attention.

It was at a typically crowded Wren party that I was first introduced to my future husband, Mike Parker. I thought him charming and amusing but, in the way of these things, soon forgot him. Some weeks later, I was playing hockey on the beach, when I came up against him in the opposing team. We were playing on bicycles so some knocks were unavoidable but one tackle from Sub-Lieutenant Parker was particularly painful. When I gave him a scolding, he invited me to the cinema. Then we started going to parties together when our off-duty periods coincided. It was not love at first sight – but it crept up on us.

Mike's ship was a minesweeper, *H.M.S. Rye*, which was still being fitted out at the Ailsa shipyard in Troon, so he had plenty of spare time on his hands. Gradually, he seemed to spend more and more of it with me. Then he was transferred to a bigger ship, a destroyer, *H.M.S. Lauderdale*, which was assigned to Atlantic convoy duties. Mike's leaves became scarcer and our time together more precious. That's when we realised we were falling in love despite the many good reasons why we shouldn't.

There was the war for a start. One did not want to fall seriously in love with someone who might be killed at any minute, although the apprehension only seemed to intensify my feelings. Then there was my father to consider. Sometimes, when I returned from an evening with Mike, I would find Father waiting up for me. At other times he would reserve his inquisition for the breakfast table. Dowdy old Troon, at long last, was an exciting place to be. I enjoyed the active scene and the bustle of life in the Wrens. I loved being in love. And besides, I argued, I was now eligible for death in the service of my country and I felt entitled to make the most of every precious minute.

It took the experience of watching my own children grow up for me to appreciate Father's concern. His possessiveness contained also a hint of jealousy. Having lost part of me to the war effort, he did not want to see me squander the rest on the first plausible young bachelor to come my way, and an Australian one at that. Mike was not regarded as an eligible prospect. During the First World War my father had served in the Argyll and Sutherland Highlanders and all the Australians he had come across shared an indiscriminate appetite for womanising. Mike – handsome, witty and intelligent – suffered from my father's innate prejudices.

John Michael Avison Parker was born on the 23rd June, 1920, in Melbourne, the son of a retired naval officer. Mike was brought up and educated in a Catholic school until joining the Royal Australian Navy at the age of fourteen. At eighteen he transferred to the Royal Navy and served on one of its most famous and powerful battleships, *H.M.S. Hood*, known in the newspapers as 'The Mighty Hood' on account of its assumed invincibility. Two weeks before it was blown up in a battle in 1941 Mike was serving on *Hood* as a midshipman. He only escaped death because a few days earlier he had left to take his Sub-Lieutenant's examination, which qualified him to be one of the youngest officers in the Royal Navy.

By the time I met him Mike had barely seen his parents for seven years. The Navy was almost the only home he knew. His parents' place was filled in England by Uncle

Brice and his wife. Uncle Brice was a surgeon-captain at the Haslar Naval Hospital at Portsmouth and Mike lived with them whenever Portsmouth was his home base. Mike was a dedicated career officer, brimming with self-confidence, and giving an impression of worldly experience and sophistication. Knowing by now that I was genuinely in love with him, I was overjoyed when he came on leave one day with a small gift box.

'I damn nearly threw it over the Forth Bridge!' he said nonchalantly. 'Aren't you going to try it on?'

Inside was a gorgeous diamond and sapphire ring. And it fitted perfectly. We kissed again and that was that – we were *engaged*!

* * *

I enjoyed being a Wren driver, especially on those occasions when Mike was a passenger, but I was growing slightly bored with travelling the same old routes time and time again. When the opportunity arose to do some relief switchboard work I accepted gratefully, which is how I came to meet James Robertson Justice.

A switchboard telephonist is at the mercy of callers on either end of the line. As a female voice, and anonymous, I was the recipient of many persuasive (and sometimes dubious) invitations, and I grew quite adept at the art of refusing them without causing offence.

One day, a call came through from the Engineering Department. While waiting for his connection the officer at the other end invited me to a party. Although I declined most diplomatically, he was roused to a booming pitch of argument – 'Right!' he roared, 'I'm coming up to see you!'

A few seconds later a great bear of a man burst into the telephone room demanding an explanation. I calmly told him that my fiancé was due that evening and that I naturally wanted to spend the first precious hours of his shore leave together with him. As it happened, Mike was early and arrived in Troon while I was still on duty. I told him about my noisy encounter with Commander Justice and in a rather uncharacteristic fit of jealousy he threatened to go and punch him on the nose.

'You can't,' I cried, 'He's practically twice your height and twice your width.'

But Mike was already out of the door. He barged his way into Jimmy's office and demanded an explanation. Jimmy rose from behind his desk and stretched to his full majestic height – 'Come on,' he said, 'calm down and have a drink.'

The outcome was that they shook hands and parted on good terms and we were both invited to the party that night.

The booming voice and the larger-than-life presence of the man was there for all to see but there was no hint, in those days, of the fame that was to come Jimmy's way when he turned to acting. After the war we lost touch with him until one night I happened to see him at a film première.

Unable to resist the temptation, I went over and touched him on the elbow – 'Do you remember me, Commander Justice?'

'Oh, my God!' he exclaimed. 'It can't be …'

A lively conversation ensued and Mike invited him to call on us. The next day the doorbell rang and when I opened it a messenger stood outside hidden behind an immense bouquet of yellow roses. The accompanying card read – 'To my favourite M.T. driver.'

* * *

Soon after our engagement, Mike was promoted to full Lieutenant. This meant an extra half-stripe on his sleeve and another transfer, to the Royal Navy base at Rosyth on the Firth of Forth. This new posting on the east coast separated us by the entire width of Scotland which meant we could only see each other when our off-duty weekends coincided. But at least we were then beyond parental scrutiny.

We used to stay at a hotel in Inverkeithing, in the shadow of the Forth Rail Bridge, where the porter had acquired a quizzical indifference to all the romantic adventures happening around him. Since the war started he had become accustomed to registering as many as sixteen different couples, all called 'Lieutenant and Mrs. Smith', in a single night. If my parents noticed any change in their daughter after these week-ends they were too discreet to mention it.

It was during Mike's time at Rosyth that he first introduced me to Prince Philip. He and Mike had both passed their Lieutenant examinations at about the same time; they were in the same 'term' to use the naval jargon. So the two youngest full Lieutenants in the Navy, were now colleagues in the same flotilla, Mike on *H.M.S Lauderdale* and Prince Philip on *H.M.S. Wallace*. They tussled like mongrels over a bone if there was the faintest whiff of spare paint in the breeze. Their ships were new Hunt class destroyers and each wanted his to be the best trimmed, most efficient vessel in the flotilla. They organised their crews into teams and challenged each other to cricket matches and bowling competitions on the green outside the Fountain Hotel in Sheerness whenever they were docked down south.

Despite their professional rivalry, Mike and Prince Philip had too much in common not to become friends. As far as the Royal Navy was concerned, they were both 'outsiders' in the sense of being foreign by birth. At the same time, being both young, ambitious and loyal, they were dedicated to the ideals of service that the Navy represented. Both of them had surrogate naval uncles ashore, keeping watch from a distance. Yet for Philip, Prince of Greece, and for Mike Parker of Melbourne, the Royal Navy was the only place they really felt at home.

So much I had learned from Mike beforehand. Then, one week-end when I was visiting Rosyth, he informed me casually that we were giving a friend of his a lift in to

Edinburgh to do some shopping – 'I've told you about him before. He's called Philip. Some sort of Greek prince. I feel sure you'll like him.'

I well remember thinking what a handsome man Philip of Greece was – tall, with piercing blue eyes and a shock of blond hair swept back from his forehead. I was not at all surprised to hear that every Wren on the base had her sights on him.

When Prince Philip came into the wardroom that Saturday afternoon, I was seated at the table, preoccupied with darning some of Mike's socks. The Prince joked that he had plenty of his own socks suffering from 'shell-shock'. I replied that if he could be bothered to bring them over (*Lauderdale* and *Wallace* were often berthed next to each other) I would be glad to oblige.

'What I can't understand about darning,' he mused, 'is where the wool goes if there is a hole in the sock.'

Not long after that brief encounter I was to meet Prince Philip again when he was included in a picnic party Mike helped to organise.

Although we were all in the middle of a war that was bleeding the Empire, I cannot recall ever having to go short of food while in the navy. When the suggestion was made one day to arrange a nocturnal picnic, Mike had no problem in scrounging the ingredients together. A mixed party of us, about half a dozen Wrens and Royal Navy officers, including Prince Philip, press-ganged some friendly Norwegians into service and they rowed us off in separate whalers shortly before dusk.

We went ashore above Inverkeithing, on the Fife bank, where the fields slope obligingly into a flattish beach. In carefree mood we collected driftwood, built a fire and started to fry a supper of sausages. There was plenty of beer to drink and the preparations were well under way when the sound of an air raid siren reached us. The truanting officers had to return to their ships as quickly as possible.

Unfortunately, the direct route back to Rosyth went through a minefield, and nobody knew exactly where it began or how far it extended. For such a short jaunt no one had thought to bring any charts. And it was growing dark fast. What had started off as a lark was turning into something a bit more worrisome. And there was another problem. It was forbidden for Wrens to be on the base after ten o'clock. The men, however, could hardly leave us to find our own way back to our various lodgings.

By the time we had scrambled our gear together and pushed off, it was inky black. The atmosphere among the Wrens was faintly hysterical. One minute we were giggling, the next shivering with apprehension, as the oars splashed and bumped against the sides of the boat. The water was calm, the night reasonably cloudless, but because of the air raid all shore lights had been extinguished. There was nothing to steer by except the gigantic girders of the of the Forth Rail Bridge against a glimmer of stars.

Somehow we managed to get back to Rosyth unscathed. Mike hid me until he had ordered a taxi. I huddled on the back seat covered by a greatcoat, while he sat looking nonchalant in the front seat next to the driver. Prince Philip, returning in the other boat, didn't want to know about this part of the escapade. We didn't know then that he had already met Princess Elizabeth as a cadet at Dartmouth Naval College and was visiting her when he was on leave. When I had offered to darn his socks nobody, not even Mike, had any idea they were being knitted for him by our future Queen.

It was inconceivable that such an eligible young officer didn't have a sweetheart somewhere, but nobody ever came close to finding out who it might be. If ever personal relationships came under discussion Prince Philip kept his to himself. He preferred to deal with people on his own terms. Even so, he was popular around the base and whenever I saw Mike and him together, the two of them were invariably larking about, navy style, in a rivalrous duel of banter.

* * *

Chapter 3

A Royal Wedding

Mike and I were married on 20th February, 1943. Because it was war-time and everything was rationed, my white chiffon dress represented many clothing coupons scrupulously saved up by my mother. I carried a bouquet of white roses, tulips, gardenias and white hyacinths. My headdress of white gardenias was held in place by a piece of Mother's wedding veil. The wedding ring was a simple gold circlet with our entwined initials inscribed inside. My bridesmaid was a friend from my schooldays who was serving in the F.A.N.Y.'s (First Aid Nursing Yeomanry). None of Mike's family was able to attend but the press reported that there was 'a sprinkling of millionaires'. Actually, the guest list was limited to my family and a few mutual friends who happened to be available in Troon and not away on war service.

From the church we moved on to the Marine Hotel

for the reception and a chocolate wedding cake. As our taxi was about to leave for the station, some of the guests hoisted Mike on to the roof. Eventually we caught the train to Edinburgh where we spent our first night of the honeymoon at the North British Hotel before continuing the next day to Pitlochry, Perthshire, and Fisher's Hotel – a beautifully preserved piece of Victoriana with faded tartan wallpaper on the walls and a stag's head in every room. We were on our own at last, man and wife. There was nobody to interfere. We went to bed early, rose late, ate, drank and enjoyed long healthy walks in the Scottish countryside. For a brief moment we were able to forget about the war.

Two weeks later, when Mike had to rejoin his ship, I received two months' compassionate leave to follow wherever he went, living in hotels at whatever happened to be the most convenient port. During one such interval Mike had to sail on an early tide before the hotel staff were awake. As he rushed off, I suddenly remembered that I had no money to pay the bill. Going to the window, I saw him come out of the front door and head for a nearby bus-stop. Somehow, I had to attract his attention – preferably without waking the other guests. I opened the window and grabbed the first thing that came to hand – a vase of tulips. As the red petals fluttered to the ground they caught the attention of a group of sailors at the bus-stop – 'Come on, sir,' one of them shouted. 'Pay the lady like a gentleman.'

With the end of my compassionate leave I went back

to Troon and the Wrens. I was posted to *H.M.S. Dinosaur* and saw the arrival of Lord Louis Mountbatten as Chief of Combined Operations. Every Wren on the base was out on parade the day he made his formal inspection. Several Wrens fainted because we were kept standing there for so long. This was my first glimpse of Prince Philip's uncle, and I recognised the strong physical resemblance between the two of them.

Mike and I continued to snatch whatever conjugal moments we could until he was posted to the Pacific Fleet. Mike, in *H.M.S. Wessex*, and Prince Philip, in *H.M.S. Whelp*, were part of the 27th Destroyer Flotilla sent to join the naval campaign against the Japanese in May 1944.

I was desolate. At the time I kissed Mike goodbye – fearing it could be for the last time – I had already left the Wrens on compassionate grounds, being pregnant with our first child. We had been married for fifteen months. During that time we had been man and wife for weekends only. Would I ever see him again?

Life in Troon resumed after a fashion. I lived with my parents, following them from one rented house to the next, *Windygates* being under naval control. Four months after Mike's departure I gave birth to a son who was christened Anthony Michael Avison, as Mike and I had agreed. Anthony was the name of Mike's pilot brother, killed when his plane crashed into a Welsh mountain during a routine training flight. But somehow the name didn't seem to fit and soon 'Tony' became 'Mike' like his father.

We wrote to each other regularly. I lived from one letter to the next in a quiet desperation of uncertainty. The closest I could bring father and son together was to paste a tiny snapshot of baby Mike on the back of one of my airmails. As for Mike's whereabouts I gleaned more from the newspapers and radio than I did from his letters. He was far too conscientious about the censorship to tell me anything precise. Not that I wanted information; just the reassurance that he was still in one piece.

Now that I was a mother, I no longer visited the Marine Hotel to party with my former Wren colleagues. Baby Michael seemed to absorb all my time and energy. Although my pregnancy had been straightforward and the birth uncomplicated, I did suffer from post-natal depression which was hardly alleviated by my anxiety for Mike. Without my mother on hand to help and advise it would have been even harder.

As baby Michael grew stronger I took up golf again and also got into the habit of going for long solitary walks along the seashore, planning for the longed-for day when Mike would return. In the meantime, he kept me posted at irregular intervals.

During shore leave in Australia, he introduced Prince Philip to his family, and together with one of Mike's twin sisters and a sister-in-law they had gone to Melbourne races. The local press, on the scent of a gossipy royal scoop, pursued them for interviews and photographs. While at sea, Mike and Prince Philip had both grown beards and they managed to confound the reporters by a neat swap of identities. Whenever the paparazzi, as they are now called, became over-intrusive Prince Philip would point at Mike and merge into the crowd with the words – 'That's the man you want.'

Mike and Prince Philip saw action off the coasts of Burma and Sumatra. The Allied Fleet was preparing for the invasion of Japan when, on the sixth of August 1945, Hiroshima was bombed. Three days later Nagasaki was obliterated. Within a week the Japanese accepted the Allies' terms and surrendered.

During these closing stages of the war I learned that Mike's health was deteriorating. Before coming home he entered hospital in Australia to have his appendix removed, but there was no immediate improvement. Thanks to his illness he missed the opportunity of accompanying Prince Philip to witness the actual signing of the Instrument of Surrender on an American battleship in Tokyo Bay.

By November 1945 Mike was back with us in Troon. Before the War I had been an schoolgirl in search of excitement. By the time it was over I had lost my former enthusiasm for adventure. I longed for a home of my own. I wanted time to get to know my husband. I wanted to grow up with a family. I wanted peace and quiet.

When Mike stepped off the train on that grey November day I hardly recognised him. His face was drawn and haggard. My joy at seeing him again was mixed with the shocked realisation that he was a sick man. Month after month Mike went to see specialist after specialist at a variety of hospitals, none of whom was able to diagnose a precise illness. He ascribed his stomach pains to ulcers brought on by the strain of combat, but the doctors could not find them.

He believed that his recovery would be speeded up by a radical change of scene and when he was invalided out of the Navy, he was set on going back to Australia to start a new life. This antagonised my parents. They had looked after me during the War. They were attached to their grandson and they had given Mike a home upon his return.

While my father continued his work in Glasgow, commuting every day as before, Mike stayed at home playing with his son and building up his strength with long walks. Unfortunately, even when Mike was on official sick leave my father resented it. When I took Mike's side, he saw it as ingratitude and both he and Mother were upset when Mike suggested we emigrate to Australia.

Finally, we reached a compromise. Mike agreed to take a job as a salesman in my grandfather's firm, the Gourock Rope Company. This meant a probationary year in their London office and a promise that he might be considered for a position as an Australian representative, operating on his own initiative. With this carrot at the end of the stick he reluctantly agreed to embark upon a career in business.

Mike moved to London, found temporary lodgings in East Molesey and knuckled down to life in Civvy Street like a million other demobilised servicemen and women. Between times, he looked for a flat suitable for a young family. I remained in Troon, travelling down with Michael as often as finances permitted.

Our life of connubial happiness had got off to a second false start. Michael, now two years old, hardly recognised his father. Mike was lonely in London and hated his work as a salesman. After his years in the Navy he bridled under the routine formalities of business life. Although he put every effort into it and was good at his job, he realised he would never be happy simply making money for somebody else. After all that he had gone through, he felt he deserved a better fate. The only thing that kept him sane, he said, was playing cricket with the local team.

We made the best of our separation not knowing how things might change for the better but always trusting that they would. One day, when Mother and I were listening to the radio while playing with baby Mike, we heard an official announcement on the BBC of the betrothal of – 'the King and Queen's dearly beloved daughter, the Princess Elizabeth, to Lieutenant Philip Mountbatten, R.N., son of the late Prince Andrew of Greece and Princess Andrew'.

Although I did not know it, that was the change we'd been hoping for.

* * *

Rumours had been circulating for months regarding Prince Philip, triggered by his adoption of British nationality in the same month as the Royal Family's departure for South Africa. Was this 'flaxen-haired Viking' to become the husband of our future Queen? Naturally, I had followed the reports with interest and immediately I heard the announcement I rang Mike to hear his reaction. After all, they had been such great friends. He agreed that we should send a telegram to his former comrade in arms – 'Many congratulations on your engagement. Best wishes for your future. Signed Mike and Eileen Parker.'

Some weeks later, a letter arrived from Prince Philip addressed to Mike, thanking us for our telegram and advising us that a formal invitation to the wedding would be forthcoming. Amazingly, it concluded – 'Whilst writing I would like to mention that I am considering getting some staff together and would like you to join this as general nanny and factotum. Yours, Philip.'

When I read this aloud to Mike on the telephone he was ecstatic at being rescued – out of the blue – from the drudgery of his London daily grind. My parents were pleased as well. All plans for emigrating to Australia were null and void. And I too was happy. With Mike doing a job that would give him fulfilment and pleasure, we might at last become more to each other than weekend acquaintances. After four long and difficult years, we would find out what marriage really meant.

Our wedding invitation arrived in October 1947. Over two thousand other guests were also on the list, mostly friends or relatives of the bride and groom. The card, gilt-edged and printed in copperplate, bore the following instructions beneath the Royal Arms:

The Lord Chamberlain is commanded by their Majesties to invite Lt. and Mrs. J.M.A. Parker to the Ceremony of the Marriage of Her Royal Highness the Princess Elizabeth, CI., with Lieutenant Philip Mountbatten, Royal Navy, in Westminster Abbey on Thursday, 20th November, 1947, at 11.30 o'clock a.m.

Dress. Civilians – Morning Dress (or Lounge Suits);

Serving Officers – Service Dress;

Ladies – Morning Dress with Hats.

An answer is requested addressed to the Lord Chamberlain, St. James's Palace. S.W.1.

Despite the pressure on accommodation in London for the Royal Wedding we were fortunate enough to secure rooms at the De Vere Hotel in Kensington, which my mother and I had used from time to time on our London visits. This time, we booked in for one week and I used the hotel as my base for my first serious exploration of London. Father stayed at home to write the cheques.

Since VJ-Day there had been little for the capital to celebrate, so this 'fairy-tale' of the English Princess who was marrying a 'Viking' was seized upon as a morale booster. It was impossible to open any newspaper without finding a picture of the future bride and groom. Every scrap of new information about the forthcoming marriage was consumed insatiably. The country needed a bit of glamour and glitz – 'A splash of colour on the hard road we have to travel' in the words of Sir Winston Churchill.

London, in 1947, was still in a state of post-war disarray with bomb craters in many of the streets. Buildings collapsed regularly just on their own. If the ruins were considered to be worth salvaging they were propped up with scaffolding. Every week brought another unexploded German bomb to light, sometimes violently. Whole streets had been Blitzed in some areas. To add to the gloom, the staples of life were still subject to rationing, although rumours abroad of Britain's straitened circumstances were perhaps more alarming than the reality. When, for instance, a new ambassador arrived from the United States, he brought with him his own supply of vitamin pills.

Despite Sir Winston's call for colour, the Socialist prime minister, Clement Attlee, had made austerity the watchword of his pioneering government and the Treasury was keeping a tight hold on the purse strings. As a very special concession, the Household Cavalry *would* be allowed to escort the Princess to her wedding in full dress but the wedding day would definitely *not* be declared a public holiday. The nation, according to Attlee, just could not afford one. It was insisted that the wedding dress conform to standard clothing regulations. Norman Hartnell was so secretive about the design for his nuptial creation he had the windows of his workroom whitewashed to discourage enterprising spies who would have paid a fortune to be able to scoop the world with a photo of the actual dress.

* * *

De Vere Hotel, Wednesday, 19th November 1947, 7.30 pm.

I didn't see Mike out as he left our room for Prince Philip's stag night at the Dorchester Hotel, I was already in bed. The glorious exertions described at the beginning of this book had left me utterly drained. I was happy for Mike and his Royal Navy chums to get up to whatever mischief they wanted so long as I got some precious sleep. There was plenty for them to celebrate, apart from the wedding. That same morning, Prince Philip, who had been plain Lieutenant Philip Mountbatten since adopting British citizenship earlier in the year, was created Baron of Greenwich, in the County of London, Earl of Merioneth and Duke of Edinburgh.

I did manage to get a few good hours of sleep before Mike was back, about one o'clock in the morning, having escorted Prince Philip home before finding his way to the De Vere. He was bursting to tell me all about what had clearly turned into quite a boisterous affair. The Press, having caught wind of what was supposed to be a 'private supper party', started pestering Prince Philip with requests for photographs. Ever since the engagement he had hardly been able to blow his nose without somebody pointing a camera at him but he hated being portrayed as a flaxen-haired Viking or some kind of celebrity knight-errant.

On this particular occasion, the eleven guests managed successfully to thwart the photographers' curiosity. Lord Louis summoned them together and said they could take as many pictures as they wanted, on one condition – that first they handed their cameras over to let the guests take pictures of the photographers. Tit for tat. After taking a few shots, the camera flashbulbs were smashed on the floor – and that put a dramatic full-stop to any further photography.

'Now it's our turn to have the last laugh,' said Prince Philip as the doors were closed, allowing the party to continue uninterrupted.

Mike told me that Lord Mountbatten represented everything he thought a Navy man should be. Between themselves Prince Philip and Mike used to refer to Lord Louis as 'the Admiral'. To have sat on such an auspicious occasion between Lord Louis (Prince Philip's uncle) and David Milford Haven (Prince Philip's cousin, his oldest boyhood friend and therefore best man) was the best start Mike could have had for his new career. It was probably one of the proudest moments of his life.

Unfortunately, for reasons best known to himself,

David Milford Haven was subsequently persuaded to write an article about Prince Philip's stag night for the *Daily Mail*. After that, relations between the groom and his best man were said to have cooled noticeably. David went on to become a regular name in London's talk-of-the-town pages thanks to a well publicised romance with the Hungarian film actress, Eva Bartok. I always found him to be courteous and amusing but, in the Household, his reputation as someone who could be trusted never recovered.

* * *

The day of the Royal Wedding dawned dry though overcast. Mike and I left the hotel at nine-thirty sharp to join a party which included three other officers from Prince Philip's flotilla. I wore a turquoise crêpe dress with matching velvet hat. Mike was in his naval uniform, looking bright but feeling rather jaded from the night before.

Our car followed the green route to Westminster Abbey, past Buckingham Palace, down the Mall, along Whitehall and up to the Great North Door. Despite the early hour, spectators were already stationed at windows and balconies along the processional route, and some were perched in trees. When we arrived at the Abbey, gentlemen ushers showed us to our seats, six rows from the front on the left side of the sanctuary. Almost as soon as we sat down we found ourselves standing again and I wondered for whom.

Not for the bride, surely. Princess Elizabeth was timed to leave the Palace at 11.03 to reach the Abbey by 11.28. Turning slightly, I glimpsed Sir Winston Churchill with his wife walking slowly down the aisle, revelling in the occasion like the showman that he was.

Briskly, in good order, the Abbey filled with guests as the sound of the crowd outside wafted through the open doors. Any minute now the groom and his best man would be arriving to take up their positions at the foot of the sanctuary steps. Meanwhile, the Royal Family had assumed their seats on the right side of the sanctuary, with foreign royalty to the left, just in front of us. From where I sat, I could see the high altar with its gold plate surrounded by a magnificent display of white flowers and green foliage.

By 11.25 Prince Philip and David Milford Haven had taken their places to await the arrival of the bride and the King. Five nervous minutes passed while the sound of cheering outside rose in volume. As Princess Elizabeth and her father entered the Abbey, trumpeters blazed into the first hymn, *Praise My Soul, the King of Heaven,* and then we saw her, radiant, with the King by her side and her retinue of pages keeping watch on the long train of her gown.

The Archbishop of Canterbury officiated and told us that the ceremony we were witnessing was 'exactly the same as it would be for any commoner who might be married this afternoon in some small country church in a remote village in the dales.' It was understandable to focus on the religious significance of the ceremony but we all knew that in every other respect this was no austerity wedding. The bride's dress shimmered with the thousands of seed pearls and crystals embroidered onto it.

The wedding reception at Buckingham Palace was strictly for members of the Royal Family and foreign royalty only. Mike and I lunched with the other naval guests at the Army & Navy Club in Piccadilly. By the time we left to go back to the hotel the crowds in the centre of London were as dense as ever. We stopped on the way to buy a newspaper reporting the departure of the newly-weds on their honeymoon, the first part of which was to be spent at the Mountbattens' country home, Broadlands, in Hampshire. Upon their return the Princess and Prince Philip (who had spent part of his honeymoon in bed with 'flu) took up temporary residence in Kensington Palace while quarters in Buckingham Palace were being prepared as their first married home. On a less elaborate scale, back in Scotland, the new developments in my own life were keeping me preoccupied.

* * *

Chapter 4

The Equerry's Wife

Mike spent the Christmas of 1947 in Troon, bringing with him tidings of comfort and joy. He had found a flat for us in London, no mean feat at a time when housing was so scarce and rents were high. Once the New Year festivities were out of the way, most of our time was taken up with finalising arrangements for the big move. It was one of the happiest Christmas holidays I could remember. It was sad to be leaving my parents but it was high time to be building a life with my husband and son.

Our first family home was a tiny flat at the top of a three-storey block in Gore Street, Kensington. It consisted of a sitting room, two bedrooms, a bathroom and a tiny kitchen so small that when the oven door was open there wasn't enough room to bend over. We could not afford to buy much furniture and most of what was available post-war was utilitarian rather than stylish. We had a few really good pieces, given as wedding presents, and my parents generously supplied other necessities. For the first few months we camped indoors on bare boards, consoling ourselves that it was a temporary arrangement and that once Mike started work at the Palace we would be able to make ourselves more comfortable.

Apart from the necessary preparatory briefings with senior Household members, Mike continued his work at the Gourock Rope Company until one day he came home with the news that he had finally received his orders to report the next day as an Equerry to Princess Elizabeth and the Duke of Edinburgh. Bright and early, he shrugged himself into the overcoat he'd been given on de-mobilisation, offered his cheek for a kiss and set off in high spirits. Within two weeks he was saying he was so busy he didn't have time even for a haircut.

Mike's enthusiasm for his new job delighted me. He was the first Australian to hold such a position in the Household and naturally, as a complete outsider, he wanted to make a good impression. He was not raised from birth in the tradition of royal service, he had no experience of Court life and no comparable education to his new courtier colleagues. But he did have a frank and easy manner and he was a quick learner. Whatever vestige remained of his Australian upbringing, he was not a stereotype of the bluff colonial with a chip on his shoulder and corks around his hat.

As a wife proud of her husband I didn't want to hinder him, nor to the best of my recollection did I ever do so, but soon I began to feel that something wasn't right. Mike's frequently repeated remark about being too busy to visit the barber was no exaggeration. By the end of the first month a clear pattern had emerged. He left Gore Street to be at the office for 9.30 and if he arrived home before the children were in bed he was frequently too rushed to eat anything I had cooked. He would rush in, kiss me, have a shave and a change of clothes, then rush out again to attend Prince Philip at an engagement.

Mike's very first task at the Palace was to help in the tidying-up after the royal wedding. There were thousands of congratulatory messages to acknowledge. People in the United States had written to offer holiday homes for the honeymoon; London Transport wanted permission to put posters of the happy couple outside every Underground station; and a woman called Ottewell had written to denounce the whole affair as an irrelevance since *she* was the rightful Queen of England and signed herself as such.

Hundreds of requests poured in for pieces of the wedding cake. Five or six of them had been baked to ensure that everyone who had been at the ceremony in Westminster Abbey received a portion. Mine duly arrived in a tiny grey and silver box, and I have kept it to this day. The marzipan is hard as a brick but the rest still looks edible.

One of Lord Mountbatten's secretaries, Nancy Lees,

was assigned to assist Mike in his chores and they spent much of their time drawing up lists of wedding presents and arranging for their dispersal, some to be put in store, some to be given to charity, and so on. All the wedding gifts, over 15,000 of them, had been on display in St. James's Palace, all neatly labelled – a chocolate-drinking set from the Pope, a loincloth from Mahatma Gandhi, a picnic-hamper from Princess Margaret...every one of them received a letter of thanks.

Given our modest circumstances, choosing a wedding present for the royal couple had presented a particular challenge – what to buy for two people who already had the best of everything? In the end, we commissioned two water colour studies of *H.M.S. Wessex* and *H.M.S. Whelp*, the two ships in which Mike, on *Wessex*, and Prince Philip, on *Whelp*, had fought together in the Pacific. I was both pleased and proud to discover in due course that these mementoes of their comradeship were later hung in Prince Philip's private sitting room.

Choosing the wedding present was merely a foretaste of what was to become a familiar conundrum. Usually when a present was required, Mike and I gave the Princess scent. *Mäjie* by Lancôme was a favourite for a long time. For Prince Philip, who had a passion for any device which would save time or provide amusement, Mike would unearth some novel piece of gadgetry.

Once, just before Princess Elizabeth's birthday, Mike telephoned me to go down to the Jacqmar salon in Mayfair and pick out a dozen of their luxury silk scarves as a present from Prince Philip. I was at a complete loss as to what might appeal because, obviously, the Princess chose her accessories and jewellery to match her wardrobe – 'Oh,' said Mike with typical airiness, 'anything with horses or dogs will do.'

I never did learn if Princess Elizabeth was ever told where those particular scarves came from but I do know that Prince Philip had a good influence on his wife's choice of clothes whereas before she had turned to her trusted maid, Bobo Macdonald.

Another of Mike's responsibilities as Equerry was to choose and order flowers for important celebrations. Every year on his wife's birthday, Prince Philip would have Mike arrange delivery of a large bouquet of white flowers, preferably lilies of the valley. Prince Philip was also good at making ingenious suggestions for jewellery. On his foreign tours, he would sometimes bring back stones to be set to his own ideas by craftsmen at Garrard's, the royal jewellers. These he would give to his wife as birthday surprises. She in turn might have a dress or a whole outfit created to set off a well-loved piece of jewellery.

To members of the Household, the Royal Family give items of silver or crystal tableware such as photograph frames or decanters, all usually inscribed with at least the Royal Cipher to identify their provenance.

* * *

The Master of the Household when Mike embarked on his palace career was Sir Piers Legh, known to us all as 'Joey'. By background and training he typified that circle of career courtiers raised from birth to manage the Crown's affairs. Joey was the son of a baron, educated at Eton and the Royal Military College at Sandhurst, then military service with the Guards. Mike's more immediate boss was Sir Harold Campbell, who had served as private secretary to the King while he was still Duke of York and was now his Equerry and Groom of the Robes. Sir Harold's particular distinction was that he was a decorated war hero. Like Mike he had served as a Royal Navy Lieutenant and survived one of the most daring actions of the First World War, an attack on the German submarine base at Zeebrugge, on St George's Day, 1918, for which he received the DSO. Understandably, given the naval connection, Mike's necessary respect for his gallant new boss was also tinged with admiration.

While 'Joey' Legh was officially Master of the Household, the King's Private Secretary, Sir Alan Lascelles, nick-named 'Tommy', also exerted a powerful influence. According to Mike, his manner could be described as pungent or sarcastic depending on one's point of view. He tended to be very short with sloppiness and bad judgement. From what I gathered, most people were a little frightened of him. He was competent and highly professional, but in most of his off-duty attitudes he was regarded as rather a dour and traditional follower of precedent.

The two new colleagues Mike got on with best were Norman Gwatkin (Clifton College, Sandhurst and the Guards) who was the Assistant Comptroller in the Lord Chamberlain's Office, and Peter Ashmore (Dartmouth Royal Naval College, Royal Navy) another equerry whose father had also been a naval officer. Norman Gwatkin was a red faced man with a thick military moustache like Tommy Lascelles, except he was more prone than Tommy to mischievous laughter and was, in fact, one of the most amusing men at the Palace. Together with Peter Ashmore, Norman provided an antidote to the prevailing very British attitude of the stiff upper lip.

Peter was younger than most of the Household, a year younger than Mike in fact, and had more understanding of ordinary life. He made a genuine effort helping Mike to learn the ropes in the palace's bewildering hierarchy. Few colleagues were ever less than polite but they regarded Mike as Prince Philip's *protégé*, and were interested to see him find his own level. Sink or swim seemed to be the general attitude.

One natural ally could have been the other obvious outsider among the palace equerries, Peter Townsend. Mike and Peter had a great deal in common. Townsend was slightly older, approaching middle age, and had served as a fighter pilot in the Royal Air Force. But he too had married a wartime bride and started a family and he too had once planned to start a new life by emigrating. Four years previously, Peter had been even more of an outsider than Mike was now. At least Mike was a personal friend of Prince Philip; Peter had been chosen at random by the RAF. Although he was charming, courteous and amiable there were those who were quite envious of him because of his bond with the King, Queen Elizabeth and Princess Margaret. Mike and he maintained a civil working relationship but for reasons perhaps best known to themselves they did not seek each other's company.

As time passed and Mike began to settle in, it was my turn, in due course, to be vetted by the Household establishment. One day I received an invitation from the Crown Equerry, Sir Dermot McMorrough Kavanagh, and his wife to take tea in the little house that came with his job at the Royal Mews. Mike had warned me what to expect so I bought a new dress to be sure of looking my best. It turned out to be a rather formal encounter, more of a quiz than a conversation. Lady Kavanagh, without making it appear too obvious, wanted to know exactly who I was and where I came from. Well groomed but nervous, I sat there balancing my cup of tea and nibbling a dry biscuit until I had passed the test.

Mike was working with so many people of high degree that it took months for me to work out who was who, and how they were all connected. In an effort to smooth the protocol, the Lord Chamberlain's Office produced a book, regularly updated, containing the names, addresses and titles of the Household members. It was easier for Mike than for myself to become absorbed in this new life, largely because Prince Philip took him completely under his wing and introduced him to all his friends. Mike repaid him with loyalty and trust. Prince Philip required nothing less. If he asked Mike a question, he expected to be provided with the right answer. Prince Philip knew how to control his temper but if aroused would express himself in forcible terms. However, if ever he did say something in the heat of the moment, he would often try to work an apology into later conversation.

The war had left Mike with an insatiable appetite for movement and variety. He lived every day for itself and he was now on familiar terms with celebrities. He was photographed with the right people in the right places. No longer was it a question of being a success in his father-in-law's business.

Above all, Mike enjoyed being himself. When the two of us were in harmony he could be the most wonderful company on earth but there was to come a point when 'being himself' took Mike further and further away from his family. Whenever he returned from a trip, especially overseas, he always brought home thoughtful presents and I knew he genuinely missed the children while he was away. Increasingly, they became my great compensation and comfort. I had friends too, of course. I went to the ballet and, in the season, we would go to the races. Nor did I neglect my golf. It did me a world of good whenever I could get out, walking for miles, concentrating on the game or sorting out the cobwebs accumulating in my mind. It could be a lonely life sometimes – the equerry's wife.

* * *

Not long after his appointment, Mike and Prince Philip set about a thorough reorganisation of their office procedures. They both had a love of gadgetry and one of their first innovations was an intercom system. Prior to this every scrap of information had to be passed by hand to other parts of the building. Mike also introduced a card index system to keep data on royal visits permanently to hand. For easy reference he had a large chart constructed on the wall of his office to show past and future engagements. Made by the R.A.F. on Mike's instructions, this chart – measuring 6ft x 4ft – was the most elaborate diary imaginable.

Whatever the workload, Prince Philip and Mike were never too busy for the occasional morale-boosting prank. Once, Mike procured a load of thunder flashes from somewhere, not tame fireworks but mini-explosives that went off with a vicious bang. He and Prince Philip used to set these off within the palace walls until the King himself complained and gave them a mild dressing down. They also held sliding competitions along the palace's polished corridors. The trick was to take a brisk run up to a mat, jump on it and maintain one's balance until it slid to a halt. Unfortunately, although a good slide would take a person quite a long way, there was no way of steering, which is how Mike once earned a rebuke by crashing into the door of the King's study.

Prince Philip and Mike went through a phase of referring to each other by comic names – 'Murgatroyd and Winterbottom will be late home tomorrow' – or – 'Murgatroyd and Winterbottom will be going out for a stroll later on'. A few times, returning from these late night strolls, they were locked out and Mike would have to give Prince Philip a hand to get him over the palace wall. Once, they went swimming in the palace pool after a late dinner and the servant in charge, never dreaming that anyone would be using the pool so late, locked them in. Only Mike's robust yelling brought another servant to their rescue.

Princess Elizabeth and Prince Philip had their own Household quite separate from the King's, although obviously there was co-ordination between the two. One of Sir Winston Churchill's younger secretaries, Jock Colville, had recently arrived to become Princess Elizabeth's Private Secretary, while a former general, Sir Frederick 'Boy' Browning, was her Comptroller.

During the week, the Princess and her husband carried out their administrative duties from Buckingham Palace. But they were newly married and wanted to be free of their obligations from time to time. Clarence House was in the process of being refurbished for them but in the meantime they wanted a place of their own where they could be with

71

friends in their own surroundings. Their first choice was Sunninghill Park, near Ascot, but this was mysteriously burnt down. Boy Browning then found Windlesham Moor for them, in leafy Surrey, and they stayed there for the first time at the end of January 1948. It was a comfortable but not particularly imposing house, set well back from the Sunningdale to Bagshot Road and hidden behind a thick screen of pines, azaleas and rhododendrons.

It was not long before Mike and I were invited to lunch with the Royal couple in their new country retreat. As we still had no car of our own we caught a train from Victoria to Sunningdale where we hired a taxi. By coincidence Prince Philip was at the front door when the taxi drove up. The driver, eyes wide with amazement, hardly recollected himself sufficiently to ask for his fare as Prince Philip greeted us. Young Michael was with us. He bowed prettily and, to my pride and relief, remained on his best behaviour throughout the remainder of the visit.

The etiquette was simple. Don't speak unless spoken to. Address a member of the Royal Family as Your Majesty or Your Royal Highness for the first time and then as Sir or Mam. Men bow briefly on entering or leaving the royal presence, women curtsey. Once again, however, I could not help feeling slightly worried about doing something wrong. The fact of Mike and Prince Philip getting on so well seemed to put pressure on me to be like that.

Mike and Prince Philip reminisced about their

wartime experiences for the benefit of the Princess, who was curious to know what Prince Philip had been like in those pre-marriage days. Tea was served by a footman, and soon afterwards the two men disappeared into the garden, where some cricket nets were set up. The Princess and I chatted about the Royal Family's recent trip to South Africa, their first overseas visit since before the war and, for the two Princesses, their initiation into the pomp and circumstance of a proper Royal tour. We also found common ground in comparing our war service. The Princess had been a subaltern in the Women's Auxiliary Territorial Service (ATS) at Camberley and, like me with the Wrens, she looked back on it with a degree of affection; she could still remember her service number. She was eighteen at the time, and driven to the motor transport depot every morning by a chauffeur for instruction in engine maintenance and driving.

All this while young Michael, good as gold and heavily sedated with ice cream, played on the floor with the corgis and Princess Margaret's little terrier. The Princess kept a bowl of sugar crystals on the coffee table and enjoyed feeding them to the dogs, who would gobble them up and wag their tails for more. Susan was the current favourite but one had to be careful; she was known to give an unexpected nip to the ankles if she was feeling moody.

When our hostess saw how taken Michael was with his new friends, she offered us one of the next litter and some months later we took delivery of a corgi pup called

Digger. He spent most of his days chewing up our furniture and the electric flex. Furniture and carpets being precious commodities at the time, I cannot say that I found this endearing. One weekend, when Mike and I were off on a sailing trip, Digger was boarded at the Royal kennels in Windsor. Upon our return the Master told us that Digger had distemper and would have to be put down. All very sad.

The relaxed Windlesham atmosphere encouraged me to feel that I was at last becoming properly involved in Mike's new life rather than being seen as a wifely attachment. All too quickly, Prince Philip ordered one of the royal cars to take us back to the station. He was concerned that we had no car of our own – it would certainly be useful – and said he would fix something up. When we were next invited down, we were driving around in Prince Philip's discarded MG sports car.

Once again, Mike and I were the only guests and the pattern followed the same as before. Lunch was a rare treat of roast beef served by a footman in Edinburgh Green livery. the Duke's personal colour. Although the servants were trained to be unobtrusive I could never forget their presence. However impassively they might stare into space, they could hear every word, and there's nothing like an audience to inhibit candid conversation. Yet I gathered enough to learn, from the Princess's appearance and other hints, that she was pregnant, whereupon I confided that I too was expecting a second child.

'Come on,' said Prince Philip, hauling Mike off to the cricket nets, 'let's leave these two to talk about babies.'

Later on, when handing round the drinks, he wagged a finger at us both – 'It should be orange juice for you two in your condition.'

Princess Elizabeth shared Prince Philip's strong wish for their children to be brought up as 'normal' as possible. Her own childhood had been confined by governesses, tutors and the impositions of war. She wished for something more ordinary for her own sons and daughters, as much freedom as was consistent with their royal destiny. And she was impatient to have those children. With them she would have acquired all she really wanted – to live in the country surrounded by lots of horses and dogs and most important of all, a family to raise. I pondered how much of a price any Princess might be willing to pay in order to bring her children up like the rest of us. When the Princess spoke wistfully of motherhood – 'I wish I could be more like you, Eileen' – I didn't feel that my own situation was quite fully understood.

The last time we visited Windlesham a Household cricket team had been organised with a fixture on Sunday in Windsor Great Park, mainly involving ex-naval friends of Prince Philip and their wives. Mike and I arrived on the Friday evening to be met by a footman who whisked our bags out of the car and up to our rooms. Another footman showed us to the drawing-room where pre-dinner cocktails were being served. Princess Margaret and Peter Townsend dropped by for drinks. When it was time to change for dinner Mike and I found our clothes and my jewellery already unpacked and laid out by a valet and maid.

We had separate bedrooms connected by a door in the manner of the royal suite. Mike's was furnished in masculine style while mine was elegantly feminine. Mike took a shower while I was faced with that ever-present problem of what to wear.

At a very early stage after moving to London I had come to the conclusion I would have to choose my wardrobe with great care. Mike's salary was £1,500 a year in addition to his small naval pension and whatever perquisites came his way. Prince Philip paid for our rates and rent from his own Civil List income. We also qualified for vegetables and milk from the Royal farms, the latter delivered in bottles bearing the Royal Cipher. My actual housekeeping money was £40 a month.

Our only additional source of income was £150 a year settled on me by my father and appropriated as a clothing allowance for me and our son Michael. I developed a policy of buying few clothes but of good quality. Most of my outfits were selected to be interchangeable with existing ones, and accessories were always chosen for versatility. Many items lasted so long I grew heartily tired of them, but simply could not afford to replace them.

Mike dressed very conservatively considering his extrovert nature. Despite his modest income he managed to patronise Prince Philip's tailor. His only concession to sartorial flamboyance in the years we were married was a loud red-check lumber jacket he was given on the Royal Tour of Canada. He always kept this in the back of the car.

Prince Philip and Mike were keen cricketers. Prince Philip had played at Gordonstoun and I heard him say that Mike was up to the English County standard as a wicketkeeper. Both of them supported the sport in every possible way and were enrolled as honorary members of a number of the more esoteric clubs. Prince Philip became Twelfth man to the Lord's Taverners, for example.

Being Scottish I had only the vaguest knowledge of cricket which is probably why, when the other week-enders went off to watch the match, I was left in charge of the dogs. They were quite well behaved at first but after a while grew restive. By the time Princess Elizabeth returned, the corgis had so thoroughly twisted their leads around my legs I was a virtual prisoner – she could not help but laugh.

After the cricket there was a supper party for those players and wives who did not have to go straight back to London. It was a cold buffet served on the sideboard. Seeing a platter filled with real stuffed eggs, a rare thing in those strictly rationed days, I served myself a liberal helping not realising that they were a separate course on the menu. When Prince Philip came to them he discovered there were too few left for the number of guests present he asked loudly who had taken them. Everyone stopped talking and looked.

Oops! If I didn't own up, perhaps one of the servants might get the blame.

'I'm sorry, Sir,' I said, blushing fiercely. 'I'm afraid I took rather too many.'

Prince Philip found my embarrassment quite amusing and for an instant I became the butt of communal laughter. It amused him when people dropped their 'aitches', socially speaking. He could also be sarcastic. I once saw him slice a pear in half and scoop out the flesh with a spoon, leaving the bare skin, as if it were an avocado. When I wondered why, he replied curtly that he thought it was a fairly normal way of dealing with a pear and that bit of the conversation went no further.

Before leaving Windlesham the next morning, at Princess Elizabeth's invitation, we were served breakfast in bed, a luxury we were seldom able to enjoy at home. When it arrived, after a discreet knock on the door from the maid, I noticed the tray cloth was embroidered with the same cipher as the bed linen; an inter-twined 'E' and 'P'. After our breakfast Mike went down first while I finished dressing. As I was leaving to catch up an unshaven Prince Philip came sauntering along the corridor in a white bathrobe. As I bobbed into a curtsey, it struck me how ludicrous the scene was, for his hairy royal knees were staring me straight in the face.

* * *

Once Mike and I were properly settled in our Gore Street flat, we started to entertain on a modest scale. Lavish parties were unthinkable as there just was no room for any larger gatherings and in any case austerity ruled the land. Mike had already started looking for a more spacious place nearby, somewhere with room for two children and perhaps a nanny. When I learned that Aunt Mora, my mother's bridesmaid and oldest friend who lived just around the corner, intended moving to the country we made inquiries and were told we could have her place in De Vere Gardens when it became vacant. With this prospect in view, we stopped adding to our furniture in Gore Street and allowed things to remain in their unimpressive state. Guests were told in advance what to expect, but mostly people dropped in unannounced.

One day the telephone rang just as I was putting supper in the oven. It was Mike, cheerfully announcing he had invited a surprise guest. I groaned – 'You can't. Supper's already made and I cannot possibly stretch it any further.'

'You'll have to,' said Mike. 'It's Prince Philip.'

I whipped my macaroni cheese out of the oven and fluffed it with a fork to make it look more generous than it was. As I popped it back in there was a knock on the door. Mike had said he would be home as soon as he could, so I went to meet him preparing a double scolding: one, for springing surprises; two, for forgetting his key. I opened the door and there stood Prince Philip. Alone.

'Hullo,' he grinned, holding out a bottle of gin. 'First

come, first served. Mike's coming later. Something cropped up.'

I took a few steps backwards and he stalked into the room with the eager walk that sometimes gave me the impression he was about to break into a sprint. The rooms were in the usual chaos. Michael had only just been tucked into bed and his clothes and toys were strewn out everywhere. Prince Philip followed me into the kitchen, and looked around (it only took five seconds) and then went to make himself at home while I rustled up the glasses. I didn't think to warn him about the standard lamp. Prince Philip sat down heavily on the chair in front of it and the shade fell on his head. He roared with laughter.

It was a bitterly cold evening and had been snowing all day. The only heating we had was a two-bar electric fire. When Mike finally did arrive, the three of us huddled in front of it, thawing out with pink gins and eating my macaroni cheese off our laps. Prince Philip seemed completely at home with what must have been meagre fare compared to Buckingham Palace. It developed into a most enjoyable evening as, once again, I recognised in our guest the affable young officer I had first met in Rosyth, full of banter and naval yarning

* * *

Chapter 5

Prince Philip In My Kitchen

Paris was the scene of the first State visit undertaken by Princess Elizabeth and the Duke of Edinburgh in May, 1948, when they were the guests of President Auriol. It was also the first major test of Mike's organisational abilities. In the years to come his talent for planning was to win him the highest praise. He always remained cool under pressure and kept his temper well. There was, however, one small incident during the preparation of the Paris trip which annoyed him intensely.

It was considered inadvisable for the Princess, so early in her pregnancy, to fly to France so the journey was to be taken by train and cross-Channel ferry. At a crucial point, when Mike was up to his eyebrows in timetables, itineraries and schedules, Margaret 'Bobo' MacDonald, the Princess's dresser, stormed in and said she wanted to know which room in the Embassy she had been allocated, and how many electric points it had and so forth.

To describe Bobo as a dresser doesn't really convey her uniquely influential position in the Royal Household. Bobo had been part of Princess Elizabeth's life since her nursery days. She was the first person the Princess saw in the morning and one of the last to see her at night. She was the only person outside the Royal Family who was allowed to called the Princess by her pet name, 'Lilibet'. No one was trusted more than Bobo and she expected the deference due. Mike had far more important things on his mind but what Bobo wanted, she was accustomed to getting, whether it inconvenienced anybody else or not.

Some members of the Household resented the way Bobo held herself aloof and exacted the full observance of strict etiquette from the servants. After Princess Elizabeth became Queen, Bobo – known to her employer as 'Mac' – was given her own apartment in Buckingham Palace with a royal car at her disposal. She ate her meals alone, not with the other domestic staff. She enjoyed the liberty of coming and going by any of the palace doors. Day-to-day visitors like myself had to use the Privy Purse door in the front courtyard.

The State visit to Paris was a great success. The ostensible purpose was to open an exhibition entitled *Eight Centuries of British Life in Paris* but, never having been there together, the Royal couple were eager to cram as much enjoyment as possible into their four days. Mike told me later that they were quite unprepared for the warmth of the welcome they received. Thousands of provincial police were drafted in to reinforce the capital's own *gendarmes*. Some of the morning and afternoon newspapers printed Union Jacks on their front pages as a welcoming tribute. Even the Gare du Nord was spring-cleaned in honour of the Royal visit.

The official engagements opened with an investiture at the Elysée Palace where the Princess was presented with the Grand Cross of the Legion of Honour and Prince Philip awarded the Croix de Guerre. From there they continued to a wreath-laying ceremony at the Arc-de-Triomphe. Mike confided to me that at this stage there came a nasty moment when the Princess looked as if she was about to faint. It was an emotional ceremony and to most spectators it most probably appeared her indisposition was due to that. Only the well-informed could have known that she was enduring the discomforts of morning sickness.

Amid the whirl of state dinners and receptions the Royal party, which in addition to Mike included Jock Colville and Lady Alice Egerton as Lady-in-Waiting, also managed to squeeze in the famous tourist attractions such as the Eiffel Tower and racing at Longchamps. They also dined privately at the Tour d'Argent restaurant, where the speciality was duck. Each bird served at the table was individually numbered. Alas, afterwards the Princess became violently ill and, as if in sympathy, Prince Philip came down with a mild attack of jaundice.

Mike came back in triumph from his first overseas visit. Paris had suddenly become the most wonderful city in the world and we would have to go at the first opportunity, perhaps to enjoy the thrill of a second honeymoon. In the meantime, there was work to do. Domestically, we had to turn Aunt Mora's flat in De Vere Gardens into a home of our own while, at the palace, Princess Elizabeth gradually cut back her public engagements because of her condition.

My own pregnancy was proceeding well. Only once do I recall suffering the discomfort of a sleepless night due to a noisy party two flights below. I complained to Mike about it when he arrived home at a late-ish hour. This incident happened during his fireworks phase. He whipped one out of his bag, lit it and tossed it into the air-well at the back of the block. In the confined space it exploded like a bomb, followed immediately by dead silence from the revellers, during which Mike gave vent to his feeling in vivid naval terms.

Shortly after we had moved into our new home Prince Philip came to lunch. This time I had been given rather more notice and, despite the rationing, had purloined a tin of American honey-baked ham, which I proudly served up with a salad and ice cream to follow. Although the new flat was a definite improvement on Gore Street, there was still no proper dining-room. Instead, we crouched at a sofa table in the front hall. The removal men had not quite completed their work and all the furniture was in the wrong places. Prince Philip gave the flat his usual thorough inspection and pronounced it suitable – 'When you are more settled, I'll come round and cook you a cheese soufflé. It's my favourite dish, but impossible to enjoy at Buckingham Palace. By the time it gets from the kitchen to the dining table, it goes flat.'

Prince Philip was very happy and relaxed that day, entertaining himself during the meal by helping little Michael use his spoon and pusher, showing both curiosity and patience with the perversities of young children. I could tell he was excited about the prospect of having children – 'It must be an extra source of fun in life ... and a new dimension to marriage.'

Prince Philip did have a cheese soufflé on a later occasion but who cooked it escapes my memory. I do remember that he had a particular interest in the art of cooking and when he moved back to Buckingham Palace after the death of the King, he had a kitchen installed in the private apartments. It was designed to be highly functional and included every type of equipment to meet one's requirements for even the most sophisticated culinary experiments. Here he used to cook his own exotic dishes with many improvisations. According to Mike, there was hardly a dish Prince Philip would not sample when they were on tour.

No one who knew the Princess and Prince Philip ever questioned that their marriage was a love match. At the time of the wedding I recall reading the occasional article suggesting that Prince Philip had 'done well for himself' but those writers too conveniently ignored what he had given up in order to become eligible. As a young wife myself I had no doubts. Princess Elizabeth was as truly in love with Prince Philip as only a woman in love can be. Moreover, she knew that in entering into matrimony her choice of partner was for life.

Prince Philip and the Princess never discussed their private life. Nor did they betray, except in the most unguarded moments, those natural signs of affection between husband and wife. I saw an occasional peck on the cheek but spontaneous affection was seldom expressed, only the occasional warm glance between them. They were absolutely determined to keep Private separate from Public. And wherever two or more of the Household were gathered together it was Public.

The Household, in turn, respected the wishes of the Royal Family. Of course, palace affairs were often the topic of conversation. There were the usual intrigues and office politics that one finds in any organisation. Yet matters of a personal nature were never revealed to strangers or outsiders. The Household presented a united front to the world and its members guarded their privileges jealously. They all believed in what the monarchy stood for. Preserving the prestige of the Crown was a common duty that over-rode any personal considerations.

* * *

Undoubtedly, there was fun to be shared in Mike's new world. In the early days he needed me by his side, often at very short notice, should the Royal couple decide on a semi-official night out. Once, Mike telephoned me at six o'clock to tell me to be at the palace by seven-thirty – 'We're going to a dance at the Dorchester'.

I had just stepped out of the bath a few seconds before. With barely time to get into an evening dress and improvise make-up, I arrived with my hair still wet and was so flustered and out of breath that I forgot the steps of one of my favourite Scottish dances, the eightsome reel. Prince Philip tactfully guided me through by taking a strong lead and, with a certain amount of pushing and pulling, he managed to steer us through safely.

Once a week there were visits to Sir Alexander Korda's private cinema in Piccadilly. On one of those occasions Mike and I met Merle Oberon, Sir Alexander's beautiful film star wife. She looked much younger than her husband, whose bushy eyebrows and heavy face gave him an air of unusual distinction. The party would normally include the King and Queen, Princess Elizabeth, Princess Margaret and sometimes the Duchess of Kent and Princess Alexandra, as well as any members of the Household who happened to be around. The Royal Family took huge delight in seeing themselves in the newsreels – 'Look at the face she's pulling!' – 'How could you wear that hat?' – 'What are you hiding from the camera there?' 'Who is that man on the left?' etc. etc.

Princess Margaret was always very sharp-witted when it came to joining in the running commentaries. She was still a teenager and loved 'breaking the rules' by propping her feet on the seat in front until reprimanded by King George. This was a regular performance she repeated week after week.

Afterwards, we would all go back to Buckingham Palace for fish and chips. The King would order his radio to be brought in. He was addicted to the radio and loved the BBC comedy, *It's That Man Again*, starring Tommy Handley.

There were also frequent visits to the theatres which were being repaired after the war-time Blitz, and slowly taking their shutters down. It was common for Prince Philip to ask Mike to book seats at very short notice. Naturally, there was never any problem in getting tickets. Again, whenever Mike telephoned me to be ready, I had to drop everything and, in my pre-nanny days, arrange a baby sitter. A car from the palace would collect me and the four of us would arrive at the theatre just as the lights were going down, to avoid recognition.

It never failed to surprise me, travelling with the Princess and Prince Philip, how little recognition they did get from the public. If the car slowed down at traffic lights, for instance, hardly anyone peered through the windows. Pedestrians who did were often so surprised they did not react quickly enough to wave or point at us. When we arrived at the theatre, Mike and I would sit one on either side with the Royal couple between us.

Princess Elizabeth was very quick at recognising other famous people. Once, I remember her whispering of one glamorous actress – 'Look, I've just seen Valerie Hobson over there' in the same tone as anyone else might have exclaimed – 'Don't look now, but the Princess is standing behind you.' On another occasion, as we were stepping out of the royal cars in Piccadilly, the Princess and I happened to be standing next to each other as the King approached, eyeing us. In our swollen condition, both being heavily pregnant, we must have looked like Tweedledum and Tweedledee.

'Who's going to be first in this race, then?' he asked with a smile.

'The Princess, Sir,' I told him. 'I'm expecting mine in the middle of December.'

'Well, if it arrives on my birthday' he remarked, thinking of December 14th, 'we'll have to have a double celebration.'

* * *

Chapter 6

'Philip's Funny Friends'

In the summer of 1948, Boy Browning invited Mike and me down to Cowes, on the Isle of Wight, to meet his wife and make use of their boat as a base for the week's sailing regatta, in which Prince Philip was due to compete. Boy's boat was called the *Fanny Rosa*. It was a refurbished fishing vessel with a proud past, having been used in the evacuation of the British Army from Dunkirk in the dark days of 1940.

Boy's wife was the novelist Daphne du Maurier, author of the bestselling novels *Rebecca* and *Jamaica Inn*. Daphne talked of her fictional characters as real people. She would often sit staring over the heads of the rest of us until, hearing something interesting in the conversation, she would swoop down from her abstractions to join in. For the really important social occasions she came up to London to be with Boy but otherwise she was perfectly content to lead her own deeply individual life at their country house, Menabilly, in Cornwall. Boy would spend the week in London in his bachelor flat, leaving for the country on Fridays. They seemed to have reached an eminently sane and civilised compromise between two very different ways of living.

Mike's days at Cowes were devoted to crewing Prince Philip's yacht, *Bluebottle*, one of the most prized of the royal wedding presents. The menfolk were eager to see how she performed under varying conditions. The other crew members included Michael Crichton, Clive Smith and Uffa Fox.

Early on, Mike took it upon himself to act as unofficial court jester and purveyor of eccentricities to Prince Philip. His most basic determination was to get as many laughs out of each day as possible while doing a sound professional job. Thus, he always had an eye open for the oddball, the eccentric character who he knew would amuse his royal employer. Princess Elizabeth nick-named them 'Philip's funny friends' and at Cowes I met the supreme example, Uffa Fox, a gross, rambling Falstaff of a man. He was partly of Norwegian origin, but was fond of referring to himself as 'just an ordinary 'ampshire lad' who had done well for himself.

Uffa's house consisted of a mongrelized collection of nooks and crannies that he had patched into the shell of the original structure. When he had first bought the place, the walls were cracked and bulging, the roof gaping open to all weathers. It was perfect for him as an exercise in his considerable powers of invention. He was particularly proud of his central heating system, which was positioned in such a manner that the water could circulate round the house without the use of a pump. Every window was eventually replaced by thick ground glass, not only for insulation against the winter gales but also so that the glazing would not distort telescopes and binoculars indoors. A lift joined the ground floor to the sail loft. When Uffa fitted a fail-safe device to it, it was one of his own design because he didn't trust anyone else's.

He was commonly acknowledged to be some sort of genius. Certainly when it came to designing boats he was a master craftsman and had designed a life-saving collapsible boat that could be attached to an aeroplane's wings. During the Second World War it saved scores of lives and provided the prototype for many subsequent improvements. Despite this Uffa didn't get one penny for his designs or hardly any recognition until Prince Philip and Mike intervened on his behalf.

Pride of the 'House that Uffa built' was the kitchen. He stoutly maintained that we are what we eat. He had two ovens and feasted regularly off joints of roast beef and thick steaks with plenty of added garlic. He also had two wheelchairs, and used to prepare his meals by wheeling himself from one range to the other according to his motto – 'Never stand when you can sit, never sit when you can lie.'

During Cowes Week he held court as the uncrowned Lord of Misrule. Any guests present would be treated to a meal of steak, washed down with bottles of red wine. To keep house for him he retained a motley crew of local wenches ranging in age from twenty-five to sixty-five. I was usually the only female guest present at Uffa's private parties. No strangers were allowed to spoil the fun, and I was only tolerated because I kept well in the background. After dinner, Uffa would regale the assembly with rude songs and stories from his vast store of nautical yarns. I once heard him boast that he had spent a day's sailing singing non-stop for a period of eight hours without repeating a single song.

That first visit to Cowes was declared to be such a success that it henceforth became a fixed date in Prince Philip's calendar. Once, Mike and I were staying in Uffa's house when he was working on the first of the Flying Fifteens, a class of sailing boat. Lurking here and there among the furniture were lumps of the early prototype. Unexpected guests were welcome to stay the night but they took their chance when it came to choosing beds. Mike and I had to use sheets that must have served several previous occupants of the bed.

Prince Philip and Mike were rejuvenated by Uffa, behaving more than ever like schoolboys. One of their pranks was to hide a bulb-operated motor-horn under a cushion. When an unsuspecting victim sat on it, there would be a loud, honking fart, greeted by gales of laughter. Another year Mike and Uffa scraped a cricket team together to play on the Bramble Bank in the Solent. It had grounded a number of ocean liners in its day, and was uncovered only rarely. The opposition was provided by a team from Parkhurst Prison, warders, not prisoners – a match which ended in victory for Mike and Uffa's team.

Princess Elizabeth never came to Uffa's house, nor did any of the other wives in the Household, except Phyllis Horsley. Indeed, after the birth of our second child, Mike decided it was better that I did not stay there and arranged for me to spend Cowes Week on a friend's boat. Regrettably, it was beached on the mudflats and forever at an angle. We slept slope-wise in our berths and I had to fry breakfast on an old biscuit tin, banging my poor head every time I turned round to crack an egg. Each morning Mike would glide across for a visit and after that, while the racing was on, we were free to explore the Isle of Wight at our own leisurely pace.

Much later on, once Cowes had become a fixture, Mike had the good fortune to become very friendly with Joe White, a dedicated yachtsman who had made his money in lemonade and was now spending it on sailing. His beautiful yacht, *The Pimpernel*, took us on annual explorations of the Brittany coastline. We would head for St. Malo, or somewhere nearby, hire cars and drive inland to an alluring spot where we would spread out the picnic hampers. Often we were able to take the children, and always Joe's wife, Edna, would be there to help keep an eye on them.

Once, when the Mayor of Deauville invited Prince Philip to see the England polo team play a United States team,

Mike arranged for *Pimpernel* to ferry him across to France. From there he flew to Balmoral and came back with Prince Philip, who brought with him, as a gift for the Mayor's table, several brace of Scottish grouse and some kippers.

* * *

Back in London after our initiation into the mysteries of Cowes Week, Mike resumed his Household duties amid a steadily growing air of excitement. The Royal baby – the first to be born in Buckingham Palace for over sixty years – was due in the middle of November. A room in the palace had been converted to an operating theatre for surgery on the King that autumn and, with an eye on future requirements, most of the equipment had been kept in place. This meant that it was possible for the Princess to have the best medical treatment without going to hospital.

Amid the excitement evoked by the pending birth, concern for the health of King George hung like a cloud over the Royal Family and the Household. With the King unable to attend to his full duties because of ill health, and with Princess Elizabeth indisposed because of her pregnancy, Prince Philip's workload increased in proportion. Princess Margaret was still a teenager and considered to be too young to embark on a full programme of public functions.

Mike was required to give Prince Philip full support during this trying period. It seemed that, day and night, he was busy with dinners, speeches, presentations and inspections. I counted myself lucky if Mike could tear himself away long enough to have dinner at home once a week. His Saturdays were more often than not spent at Buckingham Palace, so Sunday became the only day I could hope to look forward to his company.

On the evening of 14th November Mike gave me his usual call to say he would be late home. There was no need for further explanation. I already knew that Princess Elizabeth's gynaecologist had been at the palace since the previous night and the baby was due at any minute. Feeling very tired and pregnant myself I decided not to wait up but to go to bed.

At about two o'clock in the morning Mike burst into the flat and woke me with the news that the Princess had given birth to a boy and both of them were doing fine. He was brimming with eagerness to give me full details of the event. Prince Philip had been on edge all day. All public duties had been cancelled to enable him to be on hand when the birth was near. Although Princess Elizabeth was a young woman, barely 22 years old, with hardly a day's serious illness in her life, no-one was taking any chances and the moment the royal midwife called for the gynaecologist to attend the Princess, Prince Philip was also summoned. He accompanied his wife into the operating theatre then joined the King and Queen to await the outcome.

The father-to-be became more and more restive. There was nothing he could do now, except wait – something to which, by temperament, he was unaccustomed. To relieve the tension Mike suggested a game of squash. They were both good players and it had become part of their routine to round off a day's work by working up a sweat then cooling down in the palace swimming pool. They were just drying themselves when a footman came running with the news that the Princess had given birth. Their hair still wet, they both rushed up to the drawing-room where already the proud grandparents, the King and Queen, were receiving the congratulations of a relieved and happy Household.

With his usual foresight, Mike had arranged a supply of champagne and handed round the glasses while Prince Philip went in to see his wife and new son – a vigorous seven pounds and six ounces with a tuft of blond hair. Princess Elizabeth was still under the influence of the anaesthetic but by the time she was fully awake, Mike had an immense bouquet of roses and carnations ready for Prince Philip to present to her.

Outside Buckingham Palace, the celebrations began when the official communiqué was hung up on the Palace railings. All afternoon, the crowds had been swelling into their thousands. Their cheering increased when Queen Mary, summoned from Marlborough House, arrived for her first look at her first great-grandson while down at the other end of the Mall in Trafalgar Square, the fountains were dyed blue for this very special boy.

As midnight approached, the jubilant crowd showed no sign of weariness, alternating their singing of *For He's a*

Jolly Good Fellow with chants of – 'We want Philip' – 'We want Philip'. But the weather had turned very wintry and Prince Philip didn't want to expose his first born to what had become a bitterly cold night. In the end it was decided to send Mike out instead. As soon as he emerged – not onto the balcony but out into the forecourt – he was mistaken for Prince Philip and the cheering reached new heights.

Mike held up his hands to calm things down and found himself, to his amazement, facing an acquaintance, the film actor David Niven. Mike conveyed to him Prince Philip's message that the new-born Prince was doing well and that his beloved wife was fine. He continued by expressing Prince Philip's deeply-felt thanks to all who had turned out on such a cold night, and hoped that they would appreciate the need for peace and quiet; it had been a busy, trying day for all and a good night's sleep was now required.

* * *

Our daughter was born a month later, on December 16th, in our flat at De Vere Gardens. My own G.P., Dr. Peter Wingate, lived nearby and he attended. Sadly, but typically, Mike could not be present as he was on duty at the events surrounding the christening of Prince Charles. The font for that had been brought to London from Windsor and filled with water from the River Jordan. The ceremony was attended by the whole Royal Family and also the King of

Norway. The Archbishop of Canterbury officiated and the Senior Registrar from Caxton Hall attended in person. The baby was duly christened Charles Philip Arthur George.

Julie Mary Avison Parker was christened some weeks later at St. Paul's, Knightsbridge, with Prince Philip and Boy Browning as her godparents. There were four generations of my family present. Officiating was our next-door neighbour, John Jago, who the night before had been made Bishop of Bermuda.

Young Michael, who had become more and more upset by all the attention diverted from him to his new sister, decided to retaliate by tipping a bottle of nail polish all over his head just as we were due to leave for the church. We knew that Prince Philip must already be on his way to the ceremony and therefore we simply had to be on time. Somehow I managed to get baby Mike cleaned up, but I spent most of the service mentally composing a lecture on loving his baby sister. The London *Evening Star* of January 3rd, 1949, published a picture of Julie in my arms at the christening and described her 'sapphire blue eyes and fairy fingers'.

In due course, Princess Elizabeth and Prince Philip came to De Vere Gardens for drinks and to see our new home and, of course, Julie. Our flat was at the very top of the block. The lift didn't go all the way, even when it was working properly, and to reach us a further flight of stairs had to be climbed. The front porch of the building had been partly blown away by a bomb and the damage was not yet fully repaired. Access therefore was by a makeshift bridge of duckboards with a rickety railing. Answering the door, I found the Princess short of breath – 'I never thought I'd get here,' she gasped, as she came in and gratefully sat down.

Mike and I had deliberately kept Julie awake for her Royal visitors. The Princess took her in her arms and cuddled her, while saying all the nice things that mothers love to hear about their babies. We had so much of mutual interest to talk about that evening, mostly revolving around the theme of happy families. I particularly recall her asking if I had kept any of baby Mike's clothes for Julie. She herself was using some hand-me-downs for Prince Charles, including the pram which had been used twenty-two years ago for herself.

The Royal couple were accompanied by their detective who was entertained during the brief visit by our nanny, together with their chauffeur. While we were sipping our sherry, the three of them sat in the kitchen drinking beer. Needless to say, Maisie was thrilled and could barely wait for our guests to leave so that she could sit down and write to her family in Ireland.

As he did for all his godchildren, Prince Philip gave little Julie a christening present of a Bible and Prayer Book bound in red leather. Princess Elizabeth presented me with a Baby Book in which I recorded Julie's progress. On the day she was born they had also sent me a beautiful bouquet of pink flowers.

* * *

Chapter 7

Off-duty Duties

One of the first post-natal outings Princess Elizabeth made after the arrival of Prince Charles was to see how the refurbishing of Clarence House was progressing. With a son and heir to raise, the Princess and Prince Philip were more eager than ever to move into a home of their own.

Even in a period of cheese-paring stringency parliament had voted a sum of £50,000 for putting Clarence House in order, plus a Civil List allowance of £40,000 annually for the Princess and £10,000 a year for her husband. The Prime Minister, Clement Attlee, said he was convinced the country wanted a ceremonial monarchy – 'It is quite a mistake for people to imagine that the Royal family live exceedingly luxurious and easy lives,' he declared. 'The present proposals are in accordance with our approach to the monarchy today, which I believe commends itself to our people and the Commonwealth by the very fact that it is in essence a symbol of simple lives and approachable people.'

Princess Elizabeth had known Clarence House all her life as a royal residence but it was very primitive by modern standards. The building was lit by gas and there was no proper bathroom, just an enormous tub in a closet off one of the bedrooms. During the war it had been used as offices by the British Red Cross Society. When the Prince and Princess took a first look around there was rubble on the floor and the interior was shrouded in gloom – the windows were still patched with the emergency first-aid paper used for holding bomb-shattered glazing in place.

Clarence House was a mess but that's what made it so intriguing; it offered the royal couple a free hand in its re-creation. Both took a hand in drawing up the plans. At Windlesham Moor, the progress of the renovations was a continuing topic of weekend conversation. Prince Philip especially regarded it as an opportunity to apply his thorough-going pragmatism to a big project. For example, he made quite a point of getting the lighting in the kitchen to be the same as that in the dining-room – 'If they're different, the chef would be preparing food that might have a completely different complexion once it had been placed on the table!'

Princess Elizabeth, for her part, knew exactly how much of the total budget had been allocated to each item in the overall refurbishment. When estimates for the re-wiring started to come in, she was able to give Mike and me a mini-lecture on the best way of putting electricity into an old house.

As far as the interior was concerned, Princess Elizabeth and Prince Philip turned to Islay Donald, a friend of Edwina Mountbatten. She was a brilliant decorator to them both, although the Princess and Prince Philip had almost contrasting tastes. Princess Elizabeth had a pronounced preference for pastel shades; she mixed the Adam green for the dining room herself, to go with the carpet. For her sitting room she chose aquamarine walls to match the beautifully restored ceiling. The aim was to preserved all the fine original features that could be saved, while replacing the rest with the best modern alternatives. Except for Prince Philip's sitting room. He had it gutted and panelled with Canadian maplewood. Some of the panels were hinged, so that they could be folded down to provide extra working space for maps and charts.

Paintings and portraits by Laszlo and Halliday were hung on the walls. In Prince Philip's room, he gave pride of place to those two Norman Wilkinson paintings that Mike and I had chosen as wedding presents. Many of the furnishings in Clarence House were wedding gifts. It might easily have turned into a bit of a mish-mash but because the young couple put so much of their own personalities into the project, they achieved what was wanted – the comfortable, lived-in atmosphere of a proper home.

Princess Elizabeth and Prince Philip moved in on 4th July 1949 – Independence Day. For the first time, after years of courtship and marriage, they were masters in their own establishment. Their departure from Buckingham Palace brought the necessary re-organisation in the Household. Boy Browning and Mike went with the royal couple while Jock Colville remained a five-minute walk away at the palace. He stayed on for the transition before handing over to Martin Charteris. The Household at Clarence House was thus the smallest ever employed to run a major Royal residence in London. Most of the administrative work was done in the offices across the road in ancient St James's Palace – another change which undoubtedly helped preserve the homely quality of Clarence House.

* * *

Since the wedding, Prince Philip had continued his naval career, with a desk job in the Operations Division of the Admiralty. It was not exactly to his liking – 'shuffling papers from one folder to another' – but it did give him experience of the backroom work involved in running the Navy. It also provided time in which to discuss the serious matter of his future now that he was married to the heir to the throne and father of the next in line of succession.

Prince Philip's own choice was to carry on in an active service role. The Royal Navy was the life he had known and he could not understand why his career should necessarily be incompatible with marriage and a family.

His determination prevailed and he was eventually able to exchange his office desk for a staff course at the Royal Naval College, at Greenwich – a necessary step if he was to progress to higher command. Greenwich was the closest he had come to anything like a university. He would spend his weekdays there, coming home for weekends, leaving Mike responsible for running the office in the meantime.

One of the things that kept Mike busy was the National Playing Fields Association. Prince Philip was its new President and he didn't intend to be merely a prestige figurehead. With Mike in charge of the diary, Prince Philip set out to make the NPFA a test case for his future involvement in public affairs. When he addressed the committee for the very first time, he told them he had no intention whatsoever of being a 'sitting tenant'. He launched an ambitious fund-raising programme which in due course took him to the United States as well as to charity cricket matches, luncheons and dinners all over Britain. Whenever possible, he tried to open each new playing field personally. Within four years over two hundred were being inaugurated annually and wherever Prince Philip went, Mike was usually hovering somewhere near if not actually at his right-hand, giving suggestions, executing orders, smoothing the way in advance and tidying up afterwards.

The strong bond between the Prince and his equerry grew stronger with every mission accomplished. Mike revelled in it. With each new project launched and with every problem he solved his confidence grew. More and more he found himself involved with not only planning Royal visits but taking part in them.

With a new decade dawning, London was starting to emerge slowly from its enforced war-time drab. People rediscovered the art of enjoying themselves and had the money to entertain their friends. At the Café de Paris, or the Savoy, or the Caprice, we were rubbing shoulders with the rich, famous and influential. Personally, I wasn't always comfortable mingling with theatre and film celebrities. I often felt they were playing a part even when they were 'being themselves'. Among the exceptions was Jimmy Justice. His London flat was just around the corner from us and once we had renewed our war-time acquaintance, he became one of our most frequent visitors.

Whenever Jimmy's career as a character actor didn't take him away on location, he would drop in for a drink and a chat whenever he was passing. Long before we met him in Troon he had crammed a variety of experiences into his life. He had fought in the Spanish Civil War and worked as a reporter for Reuters news agency. His curiosity ranged widely and he was an amusing conversationalist. Jimmy would stop for effect in the middle of a story, take snuff in copious draughts and then wipe his nose afterwards on one of his red-checked handkerchiefs.

His social calls were most frequent during the reign of the Thursday Club, a luncheon club organised by Prince

Philip and Mike for entertaining the 'funny friends'. At this juncture in Jimmy's acting career his films were popular enough to support the expense of a house in the country as well as a pied-à-terre in London. He and his wife Dilys had bought a converted mill in Hampshire. They had a son on whom Jimmy doted. But tragedy struck one day when the boy fell into the mill pond and was drowned. Jimmy never recovered fully from this terrible blow, blaming himself for what had happened. He and Dilys eventually parted, which was another tragedy.

Gradually, Jimmy seemed to lose interest in acting – not that he ever had to act, because on set he always portrayed himself. The Jimmy I saw on the screen was identical to the one sitting next to me. To our sorrow, he retreated more and more to his estate in Scotland where he concentrated on the breeding of falcons, claiming that they understood him better than anyone else.

During this period of self-exile he would only come to London for acting jobs. Sometimes he would stay with us, other times with his mother, who was very close to him. She would listen patiently while he sat at our piano, rumbling away in that resonant drone of his. The fact that he still was a leading light in the British film industry did not impress our cleaning lady half as much as the size of his feet – 'Just look at these, Mrs. Parker,' she would gasp, holding out one of Jimmy's shoes for inspection. 'Have you ever seen anything like it?'

The world of the courtier and the world of show business had a lot in common. Mike, too, performed a glamorous role on a public stage, except that he was exposed to the popping flashbulbs of the press instead of a paying audience of fans. He was photographed with the right people in the right places and his name started to make the news. Slowly but surely, Mike was surging ahead on a path which was to lead him further and further away from me and our children. We engaged a nanny to help and I formed friendships of my own, but nevertheless the glittering moments with Mike became less and less of a consolation for my nagging sense that we were losing touch with ach other.

One of Mike's special responsibilities was to act as buffer between Prince Philip and the Press. When it came to news, editors seemed to regarded the Prince as a more legitimate target than other members of the Royal Family. When he was on duty, pressmen were acceptable; they were doing their job. On a private outing, though, they were definitely out of bounds if they attempted to get an off-the-cuff comment or a candid shot. It was up to Mike to ensure they didn't get close enough.

Privately, Prince Philip was quite a keen photographer. One day he asked Mike to take one of his cameras to Wallace Heaton's shop in Bond Street. Wallace Heaton in turn lent Mike a superb Leica camera and as much film as he wanted. Mike brought back all the equipment and started testing it on Michael, Julie and myself. When he went to fetch the developed film, he was told that some of the photography was up to professional standard and he became a sort of unofficial court photographer. Many of his pictures remained at the palace or Clarence House in the Royal Family's private albums; others he kept. A tiny Minox camera, no bigger than a box of matches, became his inseparable companion. In his years with Prince Philip, Mike must have built up the largest collection of off-duty pictures of the Royal Family ever to have been taken.

Mike's burgeoning interest in photography was nurtured by his friendship with 'Bill' Baron, one of the official court photographers. Like his main rival, Cecil Beaton, Baron specialised in soft-focus portraits of the rich and famous for which he charged thirty guineas a session. Baron had a withered arm, which forced him to crouch in a lopsided manner when getting ready to take a shot. I sat for him innumerable times and once when I was being photographed in his studio, he introduced me to a new assistant who was in charge of the lighting. The young man's name was Anthony Armstrong-Jones, the man who would eventually marry Princess Margaret.

Baron was a leading member of the 'funny friends' and their Thursday Club lunches at Wheeler's Restaurant in Soho. The apparent determination by Prince Philip to preserve some semblance of his bachelor ways with speeches, pranks and jokes was a source of friction between him and the Household's 'old guard' at Buckingham Palace. Prince

Philip was respectful towards the King and formed a close understanding with his mother-in-law, Queen Elizabeth, but he bridled at the Household's proprietorial attitude towards the Crown, its apparent resistance to new ways of doing things and its reliance on precedent in the running of royal affairs.

The move to Clarence House gave Prince Philip more freedom to run his private life as he wanted. Some of the Buckingham Palace officials feared that Prince Philip might get involved with the 'wrong sort' of people. With some cause, perhaps. Baron, for example, was hardly known as a model of propriety in the gossip columns, nor in the drawing rooms of Mayfair and Belgravia. It was one of the drawbacks of Mike's easy style that he could not always discriminate between the genuinely worthwhile and interesting characters and those hangers-on who merely wanted to attach themselves to Prince Philip for personal advantage.

Whatever the reason, both Prince Philip and Mike continued getting into scrapes in Clarence House similar to those previously perpetrated at Buckingham Palace. Once, when they had been locked out at night, they had to scramble over the gates – 'Serves them right!' commented Princess Elizabeth when she heard about it. On another occasion, one of Mike's pranks literally blew up in his face.

Carol Reed, the film director, had just completed *Outcast of the Island* and had presented Mike with a model cannon used in the production. Mike loaded it with a small charge and set it off, blowing a chunk of plaster out of the opposite wall. Intrigued by the explosive possibilities of this new toy Mike and Prince Philip placed the cannon on the desk, loaded it with another charge and stuffed strips of paper down the barrel. The next time the door opened, Princess Elizabeth walked straight into a shower of confetti.

* * *

On the whole Clarence House was a brighter and happier place than Buckingham Palace, not just because of its smaller size, which brought the Household closer together by necessity, but also because the Royal couple felt less constrained by strict protocol and their staff reciprocated the friendliness. As Comptroller to the Household, Boy Browning (Eton, Sandhurst, the Guards) was responsible for paying the bills and keeping account of the money voted by Parliament. He was a man of outstanding accomplishments, a champion athlete and sailor as well as one of the British generals later to be portrayed in the classic 1977 film about the Second World War, *A Bridge Too Far*.

In person, towards women, Boy was a paragon of charm and wit. Professionally, as an organiser, he managed to get a lot done without upsetting people. Sometimes, when Mike was off on duty with Prince Philip, Boy would kindly escort me to Covent Garden to see a performance of the Royal Ballet. After each such visit he would again start planning the one project he hadn't yet had time for – the creation of a new ballet on the theme of Joan of Arc. Sometimes we would round off the evening at the Savoy Hotel (Boy was a director of the company, like his father before him) or perhaps at the Eve nightclub just off Regent Street, handy for a drink and a light supper.

Boy's vastly greater store of experience was a stabilising influence on some of Mike's wilder schemes. He often succeeded in getting through to Mike where I had failed. His leading role in the Household continued after Princess Elizabeth became Queen, when he was appointed Treasurer to Prince Philip.

Martin Charteris (Eton, Sandhurst, the Guards) became Private Secretary to Princess Elizabeth in January 1950. He was the son of an Earl and married to the daughter of a Viscount. By the time of his appointment Martin and his wife Gay had a family of two children; Boy Browning had three children; and Mike had Michael and Julie. So, in family terms, Princess Elizabeth and Prince Philip were well served by staff who understood their own feelings on the subject.

Martin Charteris lacked the debonair glossiness of Boy's good looks – my first impression was of a rather austere personality – and his only public eccentricities seemed to be a taste for snuff and a weakness for suede shoes. Off duty he avoided the limelight and kept out of the newspapers. The one occasion I can recall Martin Charteris hitting the headlines in a big way was when his house was burgled.

It happened during a New Year's Eve party at Martin's Hampstead home. Mike and I decided to leave early and as I went into Gay's bedroom to fetch my coat, I noticed a draught coming from a window and wondered vaguely why it was open. However, as I knew Mike was impatiently waiting for me, I gave it no further thought but collected my coat and hastened to join him.

The following morning Martin telephoned to ask what time we had left. When I told him, he went on to say that every fur coat in the room had been stolen and that I, in all likelihood, had disturbed the burglars while they were at it; probably they had probably been hiding on the balcony. In the event, the crime was not discovered until Lady Rothermere went to collect her coat at 1.30 a.m. I had retrieved mine just in time but it left me with a chill to realise that the burglars may have been hiding behind the curtain when I was there.

Every morning the Princess consulted both Martin and Boy on the forthcoming events of the day and any long-term plans that required a decision. If outside advice or guidance had to be sought, it was their job to get it. They were right and left hands, respectively, men of power and influence but preferring a relative obscurity to any personal prestige. Boy had a rather more flamboyant reputation, true, but both men were equally determined that nothing should stand in the way of effective maintenance of Royal business.

Although Mike was officially Equerry-in-Waiting to both the Princess and Prince Philip, the ties of tested friendship would still have made him the Prince's man, even if the weight of work hadn't steered him in that direction. In Clarence House the innovations that Prince Philip and Mike had tried to install with only partial success at Buckingham Palace were now fully implemented. The intercom phones were set up once more and the filing system was modernised. Every time I went to Mike's office in St. James' Palace there would be new maps of Britain and the World in place. The telephones were forever ringing and any visit that lasted longer than five minutes was invariably curtailed by a buzz on the intercom. Mike never displayed anything personal on his desk, no flowers or photographs of me or the children. He did actually have a photograph of me – kept in the left-hand drawer of his desk. A reporter once described his office as being like the bridge of a warship about to go into action.

Very often I would meet Prince Philip or the Princess on visits to St. James's or Clarence House and our conversations would be polite and friendly but I was left in no doubt that office hours were for work not social chit-chats. Mike had pledged himself to the Crown. Most women expect their husband's work to take an important place in their lives but it can be desolating to feel that another family is more important to your husband than his own, and that's what seemed to be happening.

* * *

Chapter 8

Picnics at Balmoral

The Royal Family spent their summer holidays of 1949 at Balmoral as usual. Prince Philip and Princess Elizabeth accompanied the King and Queen but instead of staying at the big house they occupied Birkhall, one of the two shooting lodges on the Balmoral Estate. It was comfortable and unpretentious with a view of Loch Muick, reputedly the place where Prince Philip had made his proposal of marriage. Mike and I were invited up for the weekend with a party of other Household guests.

We caught the flight on the Friday evening and were met at Aberdeen by a small fleet of cars which ferried us through the same Deeside rivers and fields I vaguely remembered from childhood holidays with my parents. I loved fishing and was given my first rod when I was only six. My father would hire a gillie for the day who would take us out on to a loch where we'd sit for hours waiting for the fish. Once, Father took me on a special outing to Balmoral – 'to say hullo to the King and Queen' – but we got there too late and found that the King and Queen had already departed for London.

As our convoys of cars pulled up at Birkhall, the usual routine followed with servants pouring out to take our bags while others escorted us to our host and hostess who were already having drinks with some early arrivals. When the time came to change for dinner I found the bags unpacked and our evening wear neatly laid out. But something seemed to be missing – my nightgown of sheer nylon. When I did eventually find it, I discovered a large scorch right through the middle. A very flustered Bobo Macdonald later explained she had tried to iron it. Nylon was a new material at that time and Bobo, as the Princess's dresser, clearly wasn't familiar with such new-fangled man made fabrics.

The bathroom Mike and I shared contained the largest bathtub I have ever seen. When I knelt upright in it, Mike could barely see the top of my head. The water was peaty brown, wonderfully soft for bathing. There were also three washbasins, hinged so they could be tipped into a sluice underneath. In Gothic script one was labelled 'Hands', the second 'Face', and the third 'Teeth'.

Birkhall's interior was a pastiche of the Scottish Baronial style. The carpets and curtains were in either the Balmoral tartan or the Royal Stewart; the wallpaper was embellished with Queen Victoria's gold cipher. And there were stags' heads everywhere, over the doorways, on walls, in the corridors, everywhere. As I dressed for dinner I was forcefully reminded of my honeymoon in Fisher's Hotel, thirty miles to the south.

At breakfast the next morning, the Princess chose the day's menu, asking her guests for suggestions and preferences, writing it all down on a pad brought to her by a footman. Otherwise, conversation was kept to a minimum. Breakfast was the time for reading the news, especially the racing pages, and afterwards – the crossword.

The daily routine at Balmoral is devoted to hunting, shooting or fishing. At the comparatively early age of twenty-three Princess Elizabeth was already a mature stalker, having been trained from her teens by her father. Together they would go with two gillies, up into the hills. The sport consists of 'stalking' close enough to a stag to get a kill with one good shot. It demands a wily understanding of the animal and an agile alertness in keeping downwind of the beast. It also requires a keen eye and steady hand. Even at close range there is often only time to get one shot before the stag scents danger.

During that first weekend, the main sport was shooting grouse. King George VI was an excellent shot and took the keepers in hand personally when directing a shoot for his guests. The women had been warned beforehand that stout brogues and tweedy suits were the official dress for the occasion.

Having been shooting with my father since I was first able to hold a gun, I felt confident about joining the Royal party. Just after ten o'clock we set off for the rendezvous. We tramped – all of us women, including the Princess – through fields of soaking kale and turnip, flushing the grouse from cover and up into the air for the guns. I don't think I saw the King waste a single shot. Mike's loader, I noticed, had a much easier time.

By the time it came to lunch, we were soaked through to the skin. The entire party congregated in the estate's old schoolhouse where the food had been brought up for an indoor picnic. As the gillies bustled about unloading hampers, the cars were re-loaded with the morning's game for the return journey. An open fire was lit in the classroom and Prince Philip organised the women to get the meal ready – cold meat, cold grouse and heaps of salad – I was delegated to fry the potatoes in a big black pan – 'That's why we got you up here' he said.

The meal ended with cold plum pudding, a long-standing Balmoral tradition, and then we all helped to stack the plates. Again, each of us was delegated to some chore – 'Let's take the plates down to the stream,' said the King, 'and clean them up a bit. It saves the fat settling.'

I accompanied him to a nearby burn to give the plates a quick rinse and after stacking them in the hampers the men looked to their guns again, while the women were joined by the Queen and Princess Margaret who'd come down from the big house. The Queen preferred fishing to shooting and would stand in the river for hours stealthily searching for a good casting spot.

On the way back to Birkhall after the shoot I mentioned to Princess Elizabeth my previous fruitless trip to Balmoral with my father and she asked Prince Philip, who was driving, to take a detour for my benefit. The Princess pointed out interesting features to me, including the game larder, which was a small round building in the grounds just off the main drive. Here the grouse were hung waiting to be served at the royal table. Those that were not eaten on the estate were distributed to local hospitals.

We also saw an old house on the edge of Loch Muick used as a hunting lodge in the reign of Queen Victoria. The Princess offered to let Mike and me use it for our summer holidays the following year but, after thinking about it, we reluctantly declined. The ground was covered with large tree stumps and it was precariously close to the water – far too hazardous a playground for little Julie as she was then still a toddler and, unsteady on her feet, was continually getting into scrapes. It was such a pity because the Balmoral estate was a real haven in which to recuperate from the noise and stress of London.

At tea, it was a ritual for the Princess to feed her corgis personally. It turned into an almost ceremonial interlude to watch her carefully mix the ingredients on a silver tray provided by a footman. With a silver spoon she would then proceed to dish the mixture into bowls, arranged on a mat laid over the carpet.

On Sunday we all attended morning service in Crathie Church, another Balmoral tradition, watched by a large gathering of holiday makers anxious to catch a glimpse of royalty and take photographs. Then it was back for lunch and soon after that it was time to think about getting ready to depart. By this stage I had come to understand more clearly why Balmoral was one of the favourite retreats of the Royal Family. The work of the Crown went on each day but in the background; the rest of the time they were free to do what they liked best. Long walks. Lots of sport. Leisurely talks. Unhurried meals. Balmoral was a private realm where the constraints of duty were balanced by the precious freedom to simply be themselves.

* * *

Chapter 9

Boogie Woogie Riviera

In the autumn of 1949 Prince Philip went to sea again. His posting had finally come through and he was to be First Lieutenant (second in command) on a destroyer, *H.M.S. Chequers*, currently based in the Mediterranean. Uncle Dickie, Lord Mountbatten, was in command of the First Cruiser Squadron and had taken a house on the British island of Malta called the Villa Guardamangia. To enable Princess Elizabeth to be near her husband as much as possible, the proposal was made that she go out to stay at 'Villa G' for Christmas, when Prince Philip's ship would be conveniently berthed nearby.

To make the villa more comfortable for royalty, some forty cases of personal effects were shipped out in advance. Mike commuted to and from Malta, alternating periods at Clarence House with tours of duty with Prince Philip. At one point, Mike conceived a scheme to acquire a villa for us in Malta. The idea was to put me in charge of it with a view to making it the place where the Princess and the Duke could stay whenever they were together on the island.

At least Mike's trips provided extra vitamins to supplement our ration book diet. He made a point of always bringing something home with him that was unobtainable in the London shops such as oranges, onions and other Mediterranean contraband. The airport at Valetta was a breeding ground for turkeys and unfortunately, but quite often, with so many planes landing and taking off some of these poor birds would be killed. On one such occasion Mike stowed two of them under his seat. We must have been one of the few families in London that Christmas with too much turkey to eat rather than none at all.

When Princess Elizabeth went out to Malta to join Prince Philip for the Christmas holiday, she took with her the news that she was expecting another baby. Officially, it was still a closely guarded secret. Like any other expectant mother, she wanted to be the first to tell her husband personally. Her second visit was in the Spring of 1950. Bobo, as usual, accompanied her together with her two favourite footmen, Pearce and Bennett, one of whom would stand behind her chair at meal times. Apart from this small Household the Princess came the nearest she had ever been to living what could be called a normal life. As the wife of a naval officer on a foreign posting, she went to the same shops and hairdresser as all the other naval wives, and attended the same dances at the Phoenicia Hotel and the same parties within Malta's Naval society, where Prince Philip and Princess Elizabeth were known as 'the Edinburghs'.

Prince Philip, too, flourished in his sunny new surroundings. When *Chequers* wasn't on patrol duties with the Fleet, he and Mike took up snorkelling in the clear waters off Malta's coves and beaches. And Prince Philip acquired a lasting enthusiasm for polo, to which Uncle Dickie introduced him. Within four years Prince Philip was to play with a 3-goal handicap. Anything involving physical dexterity and exertion was a challenge to him. In the Flotilla's regatta, Prince Philip himself took an oar to help his ship's whaler to first place. He was fiercely competitive and wanted *his* vessel to be the first in everything. It flew the wooden rooster as the best ship in manoeuvres.

After Julie's birth I had spent a holiday in the south of France at the invitation of Cecil and Karlene Pim, friends of Boy Browning. The invitation was thoughtfully timed to coincide with the arrival of *H.M.S Chequers* in the port of Villefranche, the jewel of the French Riviera, during Fleet manoeuvres. Karlene Pim was a cousin of Mrs Herman Rogers who, together with her husband, lived in the villa next door. They had taken the Duke and Duchess of Windsor under their wing during the abdication crisis. Inevitably, when we went out for the evening, we would find ourselves frequenting the same restaurants and clubs that had been the haunts of the Windsors-in-exile. We went on daily expeditions to many of the small towns and villages tucked away from the Riviera's stream of holiday traffic.

A trip to Grasse to investigate the numerous *parfumeries* was one intoxicating adventure, followed by a refreshing swim on one of the coast's sundrenched beaches. Once, I was accosted by a handsome man who made his presence known by splashing noisily alongside me. When I stopped to tread water in order to ascertain his intentions, he offered to give me extra coaching in the breaststroke! To my utter amazement, I recognised him. It was the Hollywood actor, Errol Flynn, living up to his rakish reputation.

More elaborate entertainment than usual was arranged for the days when the Fleet was actually tied up at Villefranche. The dowager Marchioness of Milford Haven joined us for a trip to the Casino, followed by a dance at the Hotel de Paris. We were greeted by a bevy of French pressmen. We danced and gambled moderately at roulette for modest stakes, showing a small profit at the end of the evening. When we saw ourselves in the next morning's papers there was one photo of Prince Philip and the Dowager Marchioness in a slow dignified waltz next to another one of the Prince and myself in a rather more spirited attitude – 'A la Boogie-Woogie' said the caption. I showed it to Prince Philip who gave a roar of laughter and handed it round for everyone's amusement. It had been one of those rare off-duty occasions when he had been relaxed enough in public not to mind the presence of photographers.

One picnic improvised by Karlene was not quite as well-organised as the rest – a jaunt by car over the border into Italy. Early one morning, we set off with Prince Philip at the wheel and the rest of us crammed in with the picnic hampers and beach gear. It was a scintillating crisp and fragrant morning, the sun high in the sky and sparkling off the Mediterranean. We swept grandly through the coastal scenery, down towards the frontier in high spirits.

As we approached the checkpoint, Mike, in the front seat, gathered the passports together. Prince Philip's passport number was l. For his occupation he had put – 'Prince of the Royal Household'. But that was the point at which Karlene discovered she had left her own passport at home. Not to worry. Prince Philip drew up slowly by the customs patrol and gave them ample time to study his face closely. As recognition dawned, they came over and then, in a flurry of obeisance, waved us through without checking anyone's passport – 'There are some compensations in this job, after all,' said Prince Philip as we drove off with a friendly wave.

In the late summer of 1950 Prince Philip was promoted to Lieutenant-Commander and given his first command, the frigate *H.M.S. Magpie*. For this he had had to pass an examination. Mike was in Malta at the time. One afternoon, he received a message at Government House, his official base on the island. The Commander-in-Chief, Admiral Sir Arthur Power, wanted to see him.

The Admiral had a large office overlooking the Grand Harbour of Valetta. When Mike entered, he found Sir Arthur standing at the window, looking out at the busy naval scene below. In his hand were Prince Philip's marked examination papers. He had not done so well in a couple of them, putting the admiral in a quandary. Should he waive Prince Philip's low marks? All his other papers were excellent. He wanted Mike's opinion.

Mike advised the Admiral that another solution would have to be found as Prince Philip would never accept a 'cover-up'. When Mike told Prince Philip of the meeting, he had only one comment – 'If they try to fix it, I will resign.'

On *Chequers* Prince Philip had already faced the embarrassment of his own commanding officer addressing him as 'Sir'. Prince Philip felt very strongly that naval principles should be followed; respect was accorded to rank and rank was accorded to merit. He sought no special favours and, indeed, found them insulting. Mike knew Prince Philip well enough to realise he would carry out his threat and suggested a compromise. Prince Philip sat the exam again and, to no-one's surprise, passed with good marks.

For Prince Philip, earning the command of his own ship was a major achievement and it showed in his whole attitude. Later, when his wife became Queen, she was able to raise him, at the stroke of her pen, to the highest rank in all three services. In July of 1953, for instance, when the Queen reviewed the Fleet at Spithead, Prince Philip accompanied her as an Admiral of the Fleet. But I seriously doubt if it was a prouder moment than the one he experienced when he was first piped aboard *H.M.S. Magpie* as skipper.

As it happened, Prince Philip was gazetted Lieutenant-Commander on the same day that his daughter was born. I was away from London with my parents on August 11th but when I returned Mike told me how, on the night of Princess Anne's birth, he had had to go out from Clarence House to repeat the same crowd-pacifying act he had first performed on the eve of Prince Charles's birth. An elderly woman in the crowd passed him red carnation through the gate's railings as a present for the newborn baby. To a round of applause, Mike planted a kiss on her cheek to say thank you.

In later years, Mike would often say that he couldn't remember a happier period in the whole of his service with Prince Philip than the months he spent in Malta with the Royal Navy. Prince Philip worked himself and his men hard. His nickname among the crew was 'Dukey' but it was used with the utmost respect. He demanded their loyalty and efficiency and was rewarded with a well-run ship and a happy crew.

In addition to the usual Fleet exercises *Magpie* paid courtesy calls on as many friendly potentates as could be squeezed into the schedule. Prince Philip lunched and dined with Heads of State up and down the Mediterranean's shores. He also deputized as the King's personal representative at the opening of Gibraltar's Legislative Assembly.

On one tour he took Mike ashore on Corfu to attend a ceremony in the villa where he had been born. The house was modestly called *Mon Repos*. Here, on the dining room table, Prince Philip was born on 10th June, 1921, the only son of Prince Andrew and Princess Alice of Greece. He had no recollection of the place at all. At the tender age of two he had been smuggled away on a Royal Navy warship into a life of exile.

Many years later, on a holiday cruise with my second husband, we were taking part in one of those rather strained quizzes that Entertainment Officers delight in inflicting on their hapless passengers on wet afternoons. One of the questions was: 'Exactly where was Prince Philip born?' To my surprise, I was the only person present who knew the correct answer.

During the Summer of 1950 Princess Elizabeth paid yet another visit to Malta and also accompanied her husband to his homeland. As there was no suitable accommodation for her on *H.M.S Magpie*, she followed in the C-in-C's despatch vessel, *H.M.S. Surprise* with Mike on board as her equerry. By now he too had been promoted to Lieutenant-Commander. Mike and the Princess amused themselves concocting droll messages to be passed between the two ships. Biblical quotations were a favourite code. Others showed a less profound sense of wit. *Surprise* to *Magpie* – 'Princess full of beans'. *Magpie* to *Surprise* – 'Is that the best you can do for breakfast?'

As the two ships came in sight of the Greek mainland,

Mike suggested watching the dawn break over fabled Mount Parnassus. Alas, the navigating officer gave a slight dent to his career prospects by miscalculating the hour of sunrise. The Princess was awakened in the pitch black of early morning. She took it with good humour, however, and she and Mike brewed tea while waiting for the dawn to come up like thunder. She was closer now to her husband's natural environment than she had ever been and was exhilarated by the atmosphere of urgency that hangs over a warship at sea. When they finally reached Athens, Prince Philip was eager to take his wife to see his mother again. Princess Alice was in a convent there and all along the route crowds had gathered to give the young Royal couple a spontaneous welcome.

* * *

In July of 1951, barely a year after being piped aboard his first command, Prince Philip had to leave active service in the Navy. He was given an affectionate send-off by his crew, who fired a twenty-one gun salute in smoke flares. The King was ill. A bout of flu he had contracted earlier in May had not cleared up. The Royal Tour of Canada he had been due to undertake would have to go ahead with Princess Elizabeth and Prince Philip instead.

Prince Philip left the Navy on what was officially called indefinite leave. But I realized that it was more than that because Mike displayed deep pessimism and spoke of his concern that Prince Philip would never again rejoin a ship. I had become acutely aware by now that whatever Prince Philip's feelings were, they would be reflected by Mike. From Midshipman to Commander, in service across the oceans of the world, in war and in peace, the Royal Navy was all that Prince Philip had known of adult endeavour. He had grown up to call the traditions of the Navy his own. The same could be said for Mike. For them both, for the whole Royal Family and Household, life was about to change for good.

* * *

Chapter 10

On Tour in Canada

King George was now seriously ill and in September 1951 underwent an operation on his lung which took place only two days before Princess Elizabeth and Prince Philip were due to sail on the Royal Tour of Canada and the United States. Three extra days had been tacked on to the end of an already extensive itinerary in order to include a visit to Newfoundland. To have delayed the start of the tour would have shortened it into an organisational nightmare. But Princess Elizabeth was adamant that she would not leave before the operation on her father had been declared successful. At his age, in his weakened condition, there loomed the threat of a post-operational coronary. As it was, the nerves in his throat were badly affected during surgery; when his daughter came to his bedside to bid farewell his voice was barely a whisper.

To rescue the tour from collapse Prince Philip and Mike devised a solution that would allow the Princess to stay in England as long as possible and still get her to Canada on time for the official welcome. Businessmen were now crossing the Atlantic by air regularly, why not the Princess? The Government had strong reservations and baulked at the idea. Prince Philip started making loud noises about cancelling the whole thing, knowing this would bring protests from Canada's Governor-General who was responsible for the smooth running of the visit over there. It took a personal visit to the prime minister, Clement Attlee, and another to Sir Winston Churchill before Prince Philip was given approval to go ahead. As a final precaution, there was a meticulous safety briefing at Heathrow before departure.

The Household left on 7th October in a party that included Mike, Boy Browning, and Martin Charteris, with Mrs. Andrew Elphinstone as the Lady-in-Waiting. Altogether, and including a side trip to the United States, they were to be away for five weeks. As I waved farewell I had a premonition of what lay ahead in the years to come and it left me feeling dispirited.

Everything concerning the tour had been planned in minute detail. The only serious criticism from the Canadian press concerned the amount of time the Royal couple spent with dignitaries rather than ordinary citizens. Prince Philip discussed the problem with Mike who, when he wrote to me, explained the solution. A transparent 'goldfish-bowl' bubble was installed on the roof of the royal car so that more people among the crowds could see them in person.

For the Royal couple, the Canadian tour was an instructive if arduous initiation. They covered the breadth of the vast country, Atlantic to Pacific coasts *twice*, there and back, a total of over ten thousand miles, with speeches (several of them in French), prize givings and plaque unveilings at every stop along the way. At regular intervals, Mike kept in touch with Buckingham Palace so the Princess Elizabeth could encourage her father to make a speedy recovery. Mike said how moving it was to hear the King's concern in turn for his beloved Lillibet. The only time Mike felt in any danger was at the very last minute.

The Princess and Prince Philip were to sail back to Britain in the liner, *Empress of Scotland*. It lay at anchor some distance from a small inlet on the Newfoundland coast, Portugal Cove, waiting for the Royal party to make their way by tender. By the time they arrived at the jetty, a gale was blowing. Huddled together, in lashing rain, a local choir made a plucky attempt at *Auld Lang Syne* as the Royal party embarked and headed into the storm.

Each time the tender reached open water the side-winds and cross-currents pulled her towards a jagged outcrop of reef. Everyone on board hung on to whatever came to hand as the waves buffeted them from side. Then, at the fourth attempt, with the decks awash from stem to stern, the tender managed to hold her course. All on board reached the liner and were transferred safely.

When he got home, Michael and Julie could not hear enough of their father's adventures. To their delight he had brought back jeans and brightly coloured checked shirts for both children. But Mike had barely time to settle down before, within a month of his return, he had to jet off once more. This time to the other side of the world. A Spring tour of Australia had been inked into the diaries of the King and Queen but, sadly, his recovery following the lung operation was slow and he badly needed rest and nursing.

Given the success of their Canadian expedition, and given the King's reluctance to cause too much fuss, it was decided that Princess Elizabeth and Prince Philip would deputise for him overseas once again. As Martin Charteris had done for the Canadian tour, Mike was to map the terrain and prepare the way in Australia – 'Casing the joint' he called it. I had been heartbroken to hear of another separation but Mike came breezing through the door one day with the news that, because his trip was to be strictly 'unofficial' we could go with him as part of the camouflage, all of us – me, Michael and Julie.

Naturally, the prospect plunged us into a dither of excitement. How wonderful to be able to look forward to meeting the children's Australian grandparents, and being together at Christmas time – away from the English winter!

We took off from London in a B.O.A.C. Constellation

on a cold, grey morning to arrive in Sydney shortly before Christmas, having had one night on the ground at Beirut and another night in the Raffles Hotel, Singapore, where some of Mike's old friends entertained us. The journey had taken three days. Almost immediately upon our arrival Mike plunged into a whirl of briefings to gather information and crank up the protocol machine.

Wherever we went we were treated as VIPs, meeting the governors of the various Australian states and taking lunch with Field-Marshal Sir William Slim, the Governor-General. I was astounded to find that, from his photos appearing in all the newspapers, Mike was already well known in his homeland; he was even recognised in the street by complete strangers. It had been taken as a signal honour for an Australian to have been appointed equerry to Prince Philip and it had attracted a lot of attention. It almost became impossible to have such a thing as a quiet night out. When we did attempt it, we were stared and whispered about.

While Mike pursued his fact finding with the dignitaries, the three of us played on the beach. The children flourished in Australia, Sydney in particular with its carefree, open air kind of city life. As a professional courtier, however, Mike didn't want us to fall too much in love with the place – 'I hope the children don't come back with an Australian accent you could cut with a knife.'

Our stay was meant to be for three weeks but just before departure I caught measles, leaving Mike to return to London with Michael and Julie while I stayed in the care of friends. Unfortunately, our precautions were too late. Within days Mike sent a telegram – 'Children in the pink'. Yes, they had succumbed after all.

Back at his office in St. James's Palace, Mike's average working day stretched to ten and then twelve hours. King George had been warned by his doctors not to attend any public functions, which inevitably increased the demands on Princess Elizabeth and Prince Philip. The King made a supreme effort on the night prior to their departure for Australia and attended a performance with them of the musical *South Pacific*. Both he and Princess Elizabeth feared it might be their last night together, for it was an open secret that the King had cancer. Father and daughter said their final goodbyes at London Airport on the last day of January 1952.

By now I was steeling myself for yet another long parting from my husband. With a heavy heart, I travelled to Heathrow airport in the cavalcade of royal cars. Nobody, except those members of the Household going on the tour, was allowed inside the departure lounge itself. The King was closely protected in his every movement, partly to prevent the photographers capturing pictures of his haggard face, which showed all too clearly how far his illness had progressed. I caught a glimpse of him, though, as he was getting into the car for the journey back to London. I was sharing another royal car with one of the Ladies-in-Waiting and we both remarked on the King's appearance. He was ashen-faced and obviously very weak, we thought.

A pre-apprehension of his death put the whole Court under a strain. As a precaution before the Canadian tour, the Princess had been given a sealed dossier to be opened in the event of her father's death. This time, Mike told me, the Royal Standard had also been tucked away in the baggage.

The tour started with a brief stop in Kenya. The Princess and Prince Philip went straight into a day of handshakes and inspections after their four thousand mile flight to Nairobi. Thence, they went to Sagana Lodge, a hunting lodge given to them by the people of Kenya as a wedding present. Here, they were scheduled to enjoy a few days of relaxation and acclimatisation – fishing in the Sagana River, a polo match for Prince Philip and, for both of them, an all-night vigil in the Treetops Hotel up in the foothills of the Aberdare Mountains. From the verandah guests could spy on the wild game that came down at dusk to drink at the large waterhole. It was while she was at Treetops that Princess Elizabeth's father died quietly in his sleep at Sandringham and she became Queen.

The following day Mike was the first of the party to hear of the King's death. He was told by a reporter in Nairobi who had heard the news on the BBC World Service. Mike tried to get official confirmation but in the end settled for the doleful music on the radio as corroboration. He consulted Martin Charteris and they decided that the best person to tell Princess Elizabeth was Prince Philip, and the best person to tell him, was Mike Parker.

He went round by the lawn of Sagana Lodge and beckoned Prince Philip to come out into the garden. Mike broke the tragic news to him and – using her new title for the first time – asked Prince Philp to tell 'Her Majesty' the sad news. When Mike later gave me the details he said that at that moment Prince Philip looked as if the whole world had dropped on his shoulders. There is no doubt that the Queen had prepared herself for this moment, and in her bereavement bravely composed herself.

Martin and Mike now had to make hasty preparations for the journey back to England. Telegrams had to be despatched to London and also to the countries that would not now be visited. There was frenzied activity as bags were packed and gifts distributed to staff at the Lodge, including photographs, signed for the first time with 'Elizabeth R.'

Within an hour of first hearing the news, the Royal party were on the road. From Sagana the Royal party drove first to a bush landing strip. From there a flimsy plane flew them to Entebbe in Uganda, where a larger aircraft from Mombassa was due to rendezvous. Their scheduled time of arrival in London was 4.00 p.m. 7th February.

On the tarmac to welcome the new Queen were the Prime Minister, Sir Winston Churchill, and other members of the government and the opposition. Mike, who had been in charge of the whole return journey, got the timing right within thirty minutes. He spoke to me with pride about it afterwards and considered it one of his best pieces of improvisation to date. He knew then that from now on his work would acquire a greater importance and become even more demanding of his time and talent.

* * *

Back home in London I first heard the sad news in the grocer's shop at the end of our road. When I entered, the grocer, knowing of my palace connection, was unable to contain himself – 'I suppose he'll be home pretty soon, then?'

I didn't have a clue what he was talking about.

'The King,' he went on. 'He's dead. Commander Parker will be on his way back, won't he?'

I stood stunned for an instant, not quite able to take it in. Although members of the Household had kept me informed of the decline in the King's health, it was difficult to accept the fact that he was now dead. I had always found it so easy to talk to him and I knew I was going to miss him as would others, for I had known him as a kind and considerate monarch.

The King died in the early hours of 6th February, 1952. Two days later at St. James's Palace, at Charing Cross, at Temple Bar and at the Mercat Cross in Edinburgh, the heralds proclaimed the Princess Queen – 'We do hereby with one voice and Consent of Tongue and Heart publish and proclaim that the High and Mighty Princess Elizabeth Alexandra Mary is now, by the death of our late Sovereign of happy memory, become Queen Elizabeth the Second, by the Grace of God Queen of this Realm and of all Her other Realms and territories, Head of the Commonwealth, Defender of the Faith, to whom her lieges do acknowledge all faith and constant obedience, with hearty and humble affection, beseeching God, by whom Kings and Queens do reign, to bless the Royal Queen Elizabeth the Second with long and happy years to reign over us.'

For the first time in over half a century the bands played *God Save the Queen*. Flags, which had been at half mast, were hoisted high for the rest of the Proclamation Day. Meanwhile, the King lay first in the tiny church on the Sandringham Estate; then in the Westminster Great Hall at parliament. It seemed so fitting that the period of rest took place at Sandringham, where King George had been born fifty-six years previously, the second son of a second son. Now he had died there peacefully, after an afternoon's shooting – his favourite sport – and a morning watching his grandson learning to skate.

Mike and I, along with the other members of the Household bade farewell to our late Sovereign in a simple ceremony before the doors of the Great Hall were opened to the public. Every member of the Household, stood in hushed silence, head bowed in the freezing air. Scarcely any traffic noise could be heard. Nobody spoke. In the far distance we discerned a faint sound that slowly grew more distinct. It was the clatter of hooves – and the deep rumble of a gun carriage.

The King's coffin was borne in and set on the catafalque. The chaplains led the Household in prayer. Then, one by one, we filed past George VI for the last time.

The country mourned for four days. In every town, shop-fronts were dressed in black, armbands were worn and curtains drawn. In Buckingham Palace and Clarence House the Household machinery ticked over with numbed efficiency. The funeral had to be organised.

The Earl Marshal's office sent out instructions in a large envelope edged in black to everyone who was to attend. It contained passes and tickets as well as advice on dress. Women's veils, for instance, had to be of a prescribed length. Special trains were laid on to take the mourners from Paddington to Windsor for the funeral service. On the way to the station we passed through streets packed with people, all silent. The Queen, Queen Elizabeth, Queen Mary and Princess Margaret followed the coffin in a carriage. Prince Philip, the Duke of Gloucester, the exiled Duke of Windsor and the young Duke of Kent all walked behind the coffin.

On the train, all the blinds were drawn. I sat next to Daphne du Maurier and, as we had agreed earlier, we stayed together for the duration of the funeral. A congregation of about nine hundred squeezed into St. George's Chapel. All waited in the cruel cold, aware of a profound stillness. Then, as the coffin was carried in, I felt Daphne shiver and saw a mist forming in the air before her face – 'I can feel the chill of the tomb' she whispered.

The coffin, draped in the Royal Standard and bearing the crown, orb and sceptre, was taken through the chancel and placed on a purple bier. The regalia was removed and only Queen Elizabeth's spray of white flowers remained. As the service proceeded, the coffin was slowly lowered into the crypt and the Archbishop of Canterbury pronounced the solemn words of the Committal – 'Ashes to ashes, dust to dust; in sure and certain hope of the resurrection.'

With this, the Queen scattered some earth onto the coffin and the Garter King of Arms stepped forward to end the funeral with a formal recitation of the King's titles, which reminded us all of the immense responsibilities that had been thrust – and by the most personal of tragedies – into the Queen's care. When I saw the face of the Duke of Windsor as he passed along the aisle, I was startled. He was obviously finding it a great strain to control his emotions and had been unable to stop fidgeting with his tie throughout the entire ceremony.

What went on in his mind, I wondered? Undoubtedly, the burdens imposed upon George VI by Edward VII's abdication contributed to his early death. King George had worked tirelessly, in a role he neither expected nor coveted, to restore the integrity of the Monarchy in the eyes of those many British people who felt let down by the abdication of their sworn king.

As Daphne and I filed out of the chapel I noticed hundreds of wreaths and flowers on the lawn. Many were from Heads of State, organisations, etcetera, but there were just as many from ordinary subjects. One that I stooped down to examine was a simple posy of snowdrops with a scrap of paper attached – 'In memory of our sovereign'.

I wrote a letter of sympathy to our new Queen and a few days later received a personal reply in her own handwriting. She had even addressed the envelope herself. When I thought of her writing that personal note at such a very difficult time I felt profoundly touched.

* * *

The death of King George VI was followed by three months of Court mourning during which everybody took stock of their new positions. Princess Elizabeth, as Queen, obviously had to move into Buckingham Palace and Prince Philip and her two children would have to move with her; they were now 'the Royal Family'. It is traditional on the death of a monarch for all the Household to resign before being formally invited to continue. The new Queen was considerably moved by the ceremony held for the purpose, and Boy Browning confessed afterwards that he too had been close to tears.

Tommy Lascelles remained firmly in post in Buckingham Palace as Private Secretary to Her Majesty while Martin Charteris became his Assistant. Mike became Prince

Philip's Private Secretary and Boy Browning his Treasurer.

These necessary changes required Queen Elizabeth, now officially known as the Queen Mother, to swap places and move to Clarence House with Princess Margaret, and they took Peter Townsend with them as the Comptroller of their Household.

A day after the new appointments were announced I read about myself in a London newspaper – 'Happy Scots wife was today Mrs Eileen Parker, whose husband went to work at Buckingham Palace for the first time as Private Secretary, instead of Equerry, to the Duke of Edinburgh. His job means that he will be able to spend more time at his Kensington home with his wife and their two children, Michael, seven, and Julie, three ...'

Mike being Mike and his new job being Private Secretary, I was not expecting us to see much more of him, at our Kensington home or anywhere else. But it was a new year, and a new reign, and ... I could still hope, couldn't I?

Both the Queen and Prince Philip were sad and reluctant to move from Clarence House after all the work they'd invested in its refurbishment. On moving in, they had hoped it might remain their London residence for years. As I understood it, the new Queen was most unhappy to exchange her lovely home for the long corridors and echoing salons of Buckingham Palace.

For Mike and Prince Philip, the move threatened to end their less inhibited ways of doing business. There was a

154

suggestion at one point that Clarence House should remain the private residence of the Queen, using Buckingham Palace only as offices. Sir Winston Churchill, for one, was totally opposed to the idea. So the dreaded move to the palace went ahead, with the Queen and Prince Philip spending a month at Windsor during the transitional period.

For a year Sir Alan Lascelles remained as Private Secretary to the Queen until Sir Michael Adeane took over in October of 1953. He was some twenty years younger than Tommy, who was possibly too old fashioned to be completely sympathetic to a Queen who was only twenty-five herself. In fact, once Michael took over, none of the Queen's immediate entourage was over 45 years of age.

In the interim, Tommy Lascelles ensured there was a strong chain of continuity between the old and the new reigns. With regard to every major decision she had to take, the Queen's first inquiry was usually – 'What would my father have done?'

Henceforth, as Queen Elizabeth learned how to cope with her many new responsibilities, Prince Philip was officially excluded from much of her working life. From the moment of her accession to the throne, the Queen's workload increased alarmingly. In addition, she was still very much a wife and mother, and not surprisingly Prince Philip wished to assume as much of the burden as could be shared.

Alas, that point of view was not always accepted by the old guard at Buckingham Palace. It was their duty and privilege to advise the Queen personally and they jealously defended their duties and privileges.

* * *

The death of the King hit Prince Philip hard and he had another attack of jaundice. At Clarence House he had been head of the family; he made the decisions. In Buckingham Palace, he was the Queen's consort; many important decisions were beyond his control. A hundred years previously, Queen Victoria's foreign husband, Prince Albert, had found himself in a similar predicament, facing exclusion from affairs of State. Like Prince Albert before him, Prince Philip responded by building a new role for himself in public life, to go where the Queen could not, on her behalf. And in all these, Mike was Prince Philip's chief fixer.

One of their first priorities was to reorganise Buckingham Palace as a royal residence. The Prince and Mike inspected every one of the palace's rooms, over 600 of them. They extended and improved the internal communications systems and set in hand the re-decoration and re-building of the private apartments. Since he had been forced to live at the Palace, Prince Philip felt he was entitled to some say in the condition of it.

Slowly but surely, Prince Philip's public duties multiplied. The two years following the King's death saw him become President or Patron of the British Association for Commercial and Industrial Education, the British Travel Association, the English Schools Football Association, the Industrial Society, the Institute of Marketing and Sales Management, the Institute of Navigation, the National Savings Committee, the Royal Tournament, the British Amateur Athletic Board, the Historic Churches Preservation Trust, the Outward Bound Trust, the British Council for the Rehabilitation of the Disabled ... How could I wonder that Mike was never at home?

It took time for so much change, happening all at once, to settle down. In the early confusion, Mike reflected a wider gloom. Prince Philip's naval career was over. He now had to redirect his energies and learn self-discipline all over again within a different protocol, as consort to the Queen in Buckingham Palace. The old informality was gone. Even Mike had now to be announced by a footman instead of the carefree knock-and-enter of the Clarence House days.

* * *

Chapter 11

Prince Philip Wins His Wings

A grace and favour house! That was the silver lining for me when Mike and I discussed the domestic implications of his appointment as Private Secretary to Prince Philip. A grace and favour house is a Crown property held in the gift of the monarch as Head of State. The government gives such properties to cabinet ministers and senior politicians but in the Royal Household they are usual awarded to long-serving courtiers or loyal retainers of pensionable age. And since Mike was eligible for one, we investigated the possibilities

The first place we looked at was in Kensington Palace. Mike kept our car (Prince Philip's old successor to the MG, a green Zephyr) in a garage there. It was suggested that part of the palace's old stables be converted into something suitable for us but on closer inspection we decided it would prove not only inconvenient but also too expensive. Instead, we had a look at the Clockhouse of St. James's Palace, which would soon be vacant. The housing for the winding gear of the clock was right above the apartment we would be living in, so we decided to be there one lunchtime when all twelve noon chimes struck. The rooms were beautifully preserved and would have made a quaint home for us right in the heart of London. But the noise from the bell in the clock was far too loud. Consequently, we settled on a house in Launceston Place, for which Prince Philip paid the rates and rent out of his own Civil List allowance.

Our new home was an attractive Georgian house with four bedrooms. Downstairs it had a large sitting-room made cosy by two open fireplaces. Steps at the back led to a paved garden with lovely roses and various shrubs. We redecorated the kitchen with the skilful help of Islay Donald, who had designed Prince Philip's study at Clarence House. We had become regular dinner guests at her Mayfair flat so it was only natural I should turn to her when we set about redecorating.

Moving was a fairly simple matter as Launceston Place was literally round the corner from our former home in De Vere Gardens. It was purely a coincidence, but since moving down to London we had hardly lived outside a hundred yard radius from our original tiny flat.

I was thrilled with our new house and enjoyed fitting it with the motley collection of contemporary and antique furniture we had acquired along the way. No longer did our guests have to sit on the floor. Our two simple Abbey

Chairs covered with blue velvet stood in the hall. A large oil painting of me hung in the living-cum-dining room and there was also an oil of little Julie and a bust of Michael.

The painting I hung in the drawing room was one of the few portraits of me that didn't come as recognition of 'services rendered'. It was commissioned to coincide with the Queen's coronation. by *Woman's Journal* magazine which wanted a cover with a royal theme. The artist was Anna Zinkheisen and at the very first sitting we both realised we had a great deal in common. Anna was a Scot from Dumbarton, not too far from Troon, and she was such an engaging conversationalist I was sorry when the time came for her to leave after each sitting. My dress was a delicate rose-coloured chiffon with crinoline.

My next attempted portrait was less successful. In 1948, when Prince Philip wanted a miniature portrait of Princess Elizabeth painted at the time of her wedding, Mike had been directed towards a brilliant Australian painter called Stella Marks. Her portrait of the Princess, a watercolour on ivory, was a great success and became one of Prince Philip's most treasured possessions. In return for Mike's help, Stella offered to paint a similar portrait of me for nothing. I sat for her a number of times but somehow we did not have a rapport and after half-a-dozen attempts the project was abandoned.

The children were delighted with the garden in Launceston Place. The street preserved an almost rustic quietude, a stone's throw from Kensington Gardens. There was a village atmosphere about the cluster of shops on the corner. The composer, Richard Adinsell, famous for his film scores, lived in the house opposite and was often at home to theatrical personalities. Now that we had a nanny for the children, I was not as tied down as before and could accept invitations more readily. When Marilyn Monroe was in Britain making *The Prince and the Showgirl* with Laurence Olivier, Richard invited us to his house to meet her. Mike and I became regular guests at parties that could include the diverse talents of Joyce Grenfell, Clemence Dane, Joyce Carey, Merle Oberon, and others from the world of British cinema.

We always knew when Richard was at home for company. His green Rover would be parked at an angle to pavement, showing its number plate – FUN 707. Next door to him lived his close companion, a fashion designer called Victor Stiebel whose Mayfair salon was a favourite of Princess Margaret. He also worked for a time at Jacqmar where he had helped me choose the scarves for the Queen's birthday present.

Fashion-wise, Mike's royal connections could be very useful. He once came home from a dinner at which he'd been seated next to Lady Astor (the first woman to be elected to the House of Commons) to say that she had some clothes I might be interested in, as she was getting to old to do them justice. Sure enough, a day or so later Lady Astor's chauffeur duly delivered an enormous cardboard box. Amongst layers and layers of tissue paper lay a most divine pale blue, paper taffeta evening dress in crinoline style with an off-the-shoulder neckline.

I was thrilled to receive such an exquisite present and drove over to her Mayfair home with a bouquet of red roses to thank her. When I rang the doorbell, the butler came to the door and, on hearing our voices, Lady Astor appeared in person to invite me in for a chat. She brushed my thanks aside in her down-to-earth manner, saying she had been meaning to dispose of the dress any way and was only happy that I liked it as much as she did. It became one of my great favourites and I wore it frequently for several years.

More and more articles about Mike were starting to appear in newspapers and magazines, often with photos of me and the children. Consequently, we came to be recognised by total strangers. For example, I had an account at the Harvey Nichols department store in Knightsbridge, as had my mother before me. One day while filling in the account for my parcels, the saleswoman observed my name on the form and said in a stage whisper – 'Mrs *Michael* Parker? Shall I have them sent to the palace, Madam?'

I didn't like seeing myself or the children in the news by virtue of Mike's position but sometimes there were compensations in the form of gifts and perquisites. Once, we acquired a dinner-service this way, decorated to match the colour-scheme of our dining-room. My wardrobe also benefited, thanks to a very satisfactory arrangement I made with a young Scottish fashion designer called Ronald Patterson. After the mannequins in his studio had worn clothes for a photographic session or fashion show, he would lend me those that caught my fancy. He claimed it was a good advertisement for him to have his clothes seen in the right places; for me, it was a way of keeping up appearances without paying Mayfair prices. The racing at Royal Ascot was always a headache – 'What shall I wear *this* time?' Without my arrangement with Ronald I would not have been able to meet the commitment.

Mike had already taken to this newer, faster kind of life. The enjoyment of fine things was a habit he found easy to acquire. Not only did he now use the same tailor as Prince Philip but he had his shirts made in Jermyn Street and his shoes at Lobb's. Champagne was his favourite drink and, under the influence of Prince Philip, he developed a gourmet's taste for the best food. Now, when he travelled, he carried a briefcase impressed with the royal cipher as his badge of office.

* * *

With the changeover of Royal Households and the preparations for the Queen's coronation in 1952, Mike found himself so busy that an extra Equerry had to be appointed. He was Peter Horsley, a Wing-Commander in the R.A.F., who ended his career with a knighthood as an Air Marshal.

A spell at Buckingham Palace rarely constituted a threat to anyone's promotion prospects in the armed services. Theoretically, Peter was meant to deputise for Mike on those occasions when Mike could conveniently stay at home. But in fact, when Prince Philip was on an Air Force inspection, he would more often than not prefer Mike to accompany him. There was hardly anything Prince Philip did which Mike didn't know about or participate in. They even joined the Freemasons together.

Round and round span the carousel – receptions, parties, events – too often with me having to fend for myself. Many a time I had to fob off the all too friendly attentions of some man at a foreign Embassy who, on the dance floor, would mistake me for a merry grass-widow. Pete Horsley's wife, Phyllis, and I endured many such occasions together while our husbands went about their business. Without a partner even those sparkling events which at first had been such a thrill began to pall. After three or four Royal Ascots or State Banquets or Royal Command Performances they lose their appeal. It was sad because for the first few years it had been virtually impossible to go out and now that I had more freedom and the right wardrobe the most important ingredient was lacking – Mike by my side.

Buckingham Palace Garden Parties became something I tried to avoid. At about four o'clock the Royal Family would make their entrance on the terrace at the back of the Palace to be escorted in two groups to the marquees to take tea and to mingle. Along the route there and back – up one way, down the other – the three thousand guests would jostle for a closer view. Those who were especially ruthless with a sharp elbow might be rewarded with a Royal smile or a handshake. Others relied on the well-briefed ushers to bring them forward.

At one Garden Party I recall standing behind a middle-aged matron of solid build who was also rather short. As the Royal party approached, she grew so frustrated at possibly being overlooked, she grabbed the nearest chair to stand on. It had a tubular metal frame with a seat of stretched canvas. And the woman was wearing court shoes with sharp heels. As the Royal party drew abreast of where she was, I heard a loud rip as she fell through the chair and collapsed in a heap. At least she was noticed!

* * *

As if Mike's IN-tray wasn't overflowing already, in the autumn of 1952 he took up a new pursuit with Prince Philip, learning to fly. From then on flying became an obsessive hobby for both men. Any spare afternoon or morning, any odd hour that could be salvaged from other duties, was spent in the company of Prince Philip's flying instructor, Caryl Gordon, at White Waltham aerodrome near Maidenhead, handy for Windsor Castle. Not long after his first lesson, Prince Philip was able to fly himself to Sandringham for the

Christmas holidays. He was so determined to log as many hours in the air as possible, he spent the evening before his departure on the Commonwealth tour of 1953 in the air and was back in the cockpit the day after his return.

Prince Philip pored over books on aviation, made models of aeroplanes and devoured everything Caryl Gordon could possibly teach him. But there was still time left over to inject a bit of zest and fun into their activities. Prince Philip and Mike roused each other to the same mock-serious rivalry that had brought them so close together in the Royal Navy. Sometimes I would take the children out to White Waltham to see their father in the air, and I remember worrying about the idea of them enticing each other into dangerous stunts.

During that winter the cricket pitch on Smiths Lawn at Windsor became a make-shift air-field. A windsock was rigged up and the pavilion commandeered into a changing hut and briefing office. Prince Philip advanced so rapidly from his RAF Chipmunk trainer to more powerful planes that he was able to wear his wings for the Queen's Coronation. As a matter of fact, he piloted himself over to Germany to deliver some of the invitations personally. Prince Philip's rapid progress drew murmurs from the press – 'The Duke is a keen polo-player,' commented *The Spectator*, 'and there is not as far to fall from a polo-pony as from an aeroplane (or with an aeroplane) if anything should go wrong. In the eyes of the nation, and of the Commonwealth, the life of the

Duke of Edinburgh is second only to the Queen's in value and importance...'

The matter was taken up by the brass hats in the Ministry of Defence. Prince Philip and Mike used to call them, in private, 'their Airships' and were always on the alert to find ways of piercing their bureaucratic pomposity. Mike and Peter Horsley conceived the most startling sally. One day, the Air Ministry telephoned Buckingham Palace to say that a squadron of aircraft would be zooming over during the afternoon on a practice fly-past. Mike made a note of the time and rooted out an old recording of warplanes in action As the R.A.F. flew over, Peter switched on the recording while Mike telephoned the Ministry. The Palace telephones were fitted with amplification and when 'his Airship' at the other end picked up the receiver, he got the roar of machine guns in his ears – 'Listen to that,' shouted Mike, 'One of your pilots has gone mad and started strafing the Palace.'

'Oh, my God,' groaned the voice at the other end. 'Take his number ...'

To Prince Philip, learning to fly did not only offer time-saving and practical advantages, but it provided yet another challenge to his mental and physical abilities. It got him high up in the sky, miles above the photographers and hand-shakers. Aloft, he was in control and beyond interference. It must have been excellent therapy.

One of the few times I can vividly remember Mike losing his temper was on the morning of Prince Philip's second helicopter flight. It was an innocuous journey from Buckingham Palace down to Woolwich to inspect some of the troops gathering in London for the Coronation. Mike had prepared the scheme very carefully together with Prince Philip. Unfortunately, Mike chose that very morning to oversleep. He was disgusted with himself and leapt out of bed in a rage, seizing the alarm clock and throwing it straight out the window.

This scheme also landed Mike in hot water with Sir Winston Churchill, who after the general election the year before was back in Downing Street as prime minister. When Sir Winston heard that Prince Philip had made at least two trips by helicopter, he summoned Mike to see him. As Mike entered, the Prime Minister carried on working at his papers for a good while. When he eventually did look up, he gave Mike a long accusing stare – 'Is your objective the destruction of the whole of the Royal Family?'

Sir Winston took more than a statesman's necessary interest in the lives of the Queen and her husband. He rather doted on the Queen and he had come to admire Prince Philip. Under no circumstances would he tolerate the remotest possibility of exposing them to danger.

To calm Sir Winston's temper, Mike set out the case for his defence. He pointed out the amount of time that travelling by helicopter could save. He also pointed out that their safety record was good and stressed the fact that Prince Philip was already a competent solo pilot. In conclusion, he suggested boldly that Churchill try one out for himself. Mike had made discreet enquiries and discovered that Churchill had an out-of-town engagement coming up. Before going over to Downing Street he had checked with the Royal Naval Helicopter Squadron that they could have a machine ready at Churchill's disposal. Whatever Churchill may have thought about Mike's cheek, he accepted the invitation.

* * *

Chapter 12

Prince Charles At The Zoo

On 14th November 1952 the young Duke of Cornwall, Lord of the Isles and Great Steward of Scotland, better known to his mother's subjects as Prince Charles, celebrated his fourth birthday. Considering his chivalric distinctions, the Prince's party was not unduly ostentatious. About a dozen children, among them Julie, were invited to Buckingham Palace for an afternoon of fun and games in the Music Room, while outside in the forecourt the Grenadier Guards played a medley of nursery rhymes as well as Prince Charles's favourite song – *The Teddy Bears Picnic*. The corridors outside the Music Room were cleared of their statues and used for races, pass-the-parcel and musical chairs.

It was a very special occasion, however, in one other respect because it was the first time that Prince Philip was able to attend his son's birthday, and both he and the Queen had kept the day free from public engagements. It also marked another important milestone. Two days later Prince Charles was to make his first official public appearance – at a children's concert in the Royal Festival Hall.

I first saw Prince Charles at Clarence House, a sweet baby with an equally sweet nature. On my occasional visits to meet Mike I would sometimes be invited up to the Nursery by Nurse Helen Lightbody. It was a spacious room on the top floor, decorated in palest blue with scenes from a Victorian childhood on the curtains and seat covers. A large brass fireguard surrounded the hearth so snugly that busy little fingers were securely protected. Often the room would be submerged beneath drying clothes and airing laundry.

All was plain but comfortable with no unnecessary frills. There was a sawn-off desk for Prince Charles and a deal table dominating the centre of the room. Toys were kept in a glass-fronted dresser on one side of the fireplace while a radiogram stood on the other side.

The Nursery also served as a sitting room for staff. Nurse Lightbody was the senior nanny and had Mabel Anderson as her assistant. A Nursery footman brought meals up from the kitchen. A proper Nursery kitchen was not installed until Princess Anne was born. This mini-Household was to be expanded the following year to include Miss Katherine Peebles as governess.

Katherine Peebles was a Scot like Bobo Macdonald, a shrewd, humorous woman who displayed a firm and astute hand with the children. They called her 'Mispy' which was their affectionate version of 'Miss P'. The Queen and Prince Philip wanted to have as much contact with their children as possible. At Clarence House, a half-hour after breakfast and an hour or more at bath-time was set aside as family time. True to her oft-stated intentions, the Queen tried to ensure that both children were brought up as 'normally' as possible considering their position. They were taught to be polite to servants and they were scolded and spanked when necessary. The staff called Prince Charles and Princess Anne by their Christian names. As far as I could tell, they really did spend their first years oblivious of the fact that they were quite different from other children.

They called Prince Philip 'Papa', their mother 'Mama' and the Queen Mother 'Gan-Gan'. Neither child was materially spoiled. It was almost a matter of principle that Anne wore some of her brother's cast-off clothes, suitably altered. The boring bits of being royal – the shadowing by detectives, the lack of personal privacy – were also accepted as a matter of course. Anne was more mischievous than her brother. When she realised that the sentries went through the same fascinating procedure of presenting arms every time she passed, she began to do it for a lark. That is, until she was called sharply to attention herself by Mispy.

Charles grew into a shy, thoughtful and well-mannered young boy. Anne was the one who took decidedly after her father, although her brother had inherited Prince Philip's blond colouring. I was in the Nursery one day when Nurse Lightbody was packing a pair of his shoes to send to the cobbler's. She explained that they had to be specially altered to cure Charles's knock-knees (inherited from his grandfather, George VI). He was also 'chesty' and prone to niggling coughs and throat ailments. As soon as Charles was old enough, Prince Philip started to teach him to swim. Nurse Lightbody was often overruled when voicing concern over the possible ill effects of a swim on Charles's health.

It wasn't until after the Princess became Queen that I began to know the Royal children well. At Buckingham Palace a new Nursery was installed on the floor above the private apartments. Sometimes it resembled a menagerie more than a nursery. In addition to the corgis, there were caged songbirds (Annie and David), at least one hamster and a white fluffy rabbit called Harvey. Charles and Anne had to look after these animals themselves as part of the daily chores.

It was to this palace nursery that I took Julie for the Thursday afternoon dancing classes, led by Miss Betty Vacani (in real life she was a plumpish Mrs Rankin) to whose dance school both Princess Elizabeth and Princess Margaret had been sent at the same age. The class included some of Charles's friends as well as children of the Household. The Neville children would usually be there, David Penn, the two sons of Lady Margaret Hay and Viscount Lascelles.

Julie took to dancing quite naturally. She picked up steps quickly and exhibited a flair for timing and rhythm.

I was soon paying Miss Vacani for extra tuition. This had the rather embarrassing effect of making Julie the star pupil on Thursday afternoons. Whenever Miss Vacani wanted to introduce the class to a new dance, it was Julie she called out to demonstrate. When it came time to choose partners, Julie was usually the first choice and Prince Charles made a bee-line for her.

Julie was quite innocent of causing a stir but it was all too obvious to the adults that Prince Charles was forming an attachment. It was especially noticeable whenever he asked for Julie to be allowed to stay on after dancing for nursery tea. Charles, Anne and Julie would play in the garden while I chatted to Nurse Lightbody and Mabel Anderson. Charles and Julie were such good company for each other that 'staying on for tea' happened quite regularly and sometimes I would be able to drop Julie at the palace while I went shopping.

I wanted to reciprocate the hospitality Julie was receiving at the palace but that was only possible once we had moved to Launceston Place. Mike and I furnished a nursery for our own children down in the basement and the Royal children began to come for tea. They both had masses of toys at the palace but Michael and Julie's toys were different and, like most children, the Prince and Princess enjoyed a change. Anne, in particular, insisted on emptying both of the large toy cupboards that flanked the fireplace. If Nurse Lightbody reprimanded her and told her she was not to have any more toys, Princess Anne would plead –

'Just one more, that one over there' – and point to the most inaccessible shelf.

There was only a month separating Charles and Julie in age. They were a delightful little pair, well matched in temperament as well as on the dance floor. Their friendship caught the attention of the American press. Under the headline – 'Fast Driver Like Father Charles Shows off Skill To Beautiful Brunette' – one reporter indulged in a wildly premature attempt at match-making – 'Prince Charles would be more excited about the coronation of his mother next Tuesday but it's spring and like many another young man his fancy has lightly turned to another matter. Her name is Julie Parker. She is a brunette with big blue eyes. She is four and a half and beautiful. Prince Charles … is the masterful type. Experts in these matters say the romance isn't all one-sided. Prince Charles started out showing Julie his pet rabbit. Then he drove her round in his light blue pedal car. Julie was impressed by Charles's dare-devil tactics. She gave a toy model of a milk truck. Charles collects this kind of toy. Later she bought him a toy jeep. Prince Charles gave her a ride seated on the hood of his car – an unprecedented honour …'

Reminiscing back to the nursery days in Buckingham Palace, I remember that the Wendy house was often the focus of noisy disputes. Princess Anne would lock herself in, leaving the other two outside, trying to kick the door down, until the rumpus grew so loud that we adults had to intervene. There were the usual childish tantrums and petulance, but nothing that couldn't be cured by a sharp word, usually intended for Princess Anne who was by far the more boisterous. She showed a tendency to dominate her older brother. They had, between them, a bicycle and a tricycle. Whichever one Charles wanted, Anne would covet. And when she became really worked up, she would start throwing things.

Once, Mike and I took Prince Charles, Princess Anne and Julie to London Zoo on a private outing chaperoned by Mabel Anderson. It was on a rainy Sunday morning when the Zoo was only open to Fellows of the Zoological Society. Hardly anyone recognised the heir to the throne as the children scampered around with complete freedom among the various animal cages, squealing with delight at the antics of the monkeys. I cannot say who were more exhausted by the end of this happy outing, the three adults or the three children.

On Coronation Day, Prince Charles hosted a party for fourteen children, mostly Household, to watch the ceremony on television. Television sets were specially installed in one of the three great lounges of the Queen's private suite on the first floor of Buckingham Palace overlooking the Mall. When they tired of the TV, there were orange boxes covered with scarlet carpet on the balcony so they could view the spectacle below. In addition to Michael and Julie, there were Max and Louise, the children of Helene Cordet (a French-born actress and cabaret star), David Lascelles, David Penn,

Lady Sarah Winnington, Lady Henrietta Fitzroy, the two Hay children, and Marilyn Wills.

When it was time for Prince Charles to go to Westminster Abbey to take part in the ceremony, his guests remained well looked after. A butler and five waiters had been assigned to attend the buffet. By special request from Julie, blackcurrant juice was served as well as ice-cream, fizzy lemonade and cakes.

Upon the Queen's return from the Abbey she looked in on the children who had been drilled by anxious parents to receive Her Majesty with solemn bows and curtseys. That night when I asked Julie what the Queen had looked like on television she summed up the whole day perfectly – 'Mummy, she was sparkling all over!'

I suppose the most poignant of my memories of the young Prince Charles came later, when Mike took us with him to reconnoitre the Royal tour of Australia under the cover of a family visit to Melbourne. The regular dancing class at Buckingham Palace took place the day before our departure. This time, when the lesson was over, the children stayed on for what turned out to be a farewell tea party for Julie. Afterwards, making our farewell, Prince Charles looked at Nurse Lightbody – 'May I kiss Julie goodbye?'

After giving Julie a solemn kiss the cheek he then turned to me – 'Now, may I kiss her Mama?'

I offered my cheek in a suitably adult fashion and then shook hands. It seemed charming, almost quaint, but it revealed something more. Prince Charles, I perceived, was already turning into quite a serious young man. He lived in a palace, with a throne, and it was destined to be his.

* * *

Chapter 13

Behind The Scenes At The Coronation

I'm not sure if the Coronation fever of 1953 gripped the entire British nation, but it certainly held the whole of London in thrall as, month by month, the city's war-scarred fabric was spruced up for the celebrations. For weeks beforehand, along the processional route, streets were blocked off so that the people taking part could be rehearsed in meticulous detail. Mike's constant companion was his monogrammed briefcase, bulging with sheaves of timetables and plans. Seldom during those arduous months could he snatch a moment with his family. Now and then, as he sat over his papers, I would pick up bits of information on how the things were progressing and it always confirmed the same thing; the crowning of our new Queen was going to be the biggest Royal extravaganza of the century. Some were predicting hopefully that it marked the inauguration of a new Elizabethan age.

According to doctrine, Princess Elizabeth became Queen at the moment of her father's death, yet it was not until June of the following year, 1953, that she was crowned. Traditionally, the organisation of the Coronation is in the hands of the Earl Marshal of England, the Duke of Norfolk. I met him in Boy Browning's office in the early days of the preparations and I well recall the suggestion of Sir Norman Gwatkin, who was also present – 'Let's look at an old copy of the *Illustrated London News* and see what they did last time.'

To assist the Duke of Norfolk a Coronation Commission was appointed with Prince Philip as the chairman. Other members included the Archbishop of Canterbury, the Prime Minister, Sir Winston Churchill, and the Minister of Works, Sir David Eccles. Representatives from Canada, Australia, South Africa, Pakistan and Ceylon were also brought in to reflect the wider interests of the Commonwealth. The task facing the Minister of Works was to supply sufficient men and materials for transforming the processional route from Buckingham Palace to Westminster Abbey into one vast pageant, not only for the huge audience expected to attend in person but also for the millions more who would be watching on television screens. In the end, 700 miles of tubing was used in the scaffolding and enough paint to cover the Forth Rail Bridge from end to end. And somewhere, Mike assured me, ten acres of flowers had been planted to ensure that they would be in full bloom by the beginning of June.

While all this was going on, Buckingham Palace was

busy putting its own house in order. The Ballroom was marked with tape to indicate the approximate shape of Westminster Abbey. Household members assumed the role of the chief actors and the Queen herself, with a sheet pinned to her shoulders, went through tiring rehearsals time and again. Nothing less than perfect was acceptable. After one such rehearsal Mike came home and proclaimed in a nonchalant manner that he had only minutes before been carrying the Imperial State Crown. The children used to hang on his every word.

It was impossible to work in the Household without believing that pomp and circumstance was necessary to put a shine on the Crown's prestige. But what Prince Philip so intensely disliked was the need to perform like some fairground freak. Mike always said Prince Philip bristled like a grizzly bear whenever a photographer had an appointment. A surprising number of official photographs were continuously on the agenda – for changes of uniform, promotions, new appointments, anniversaries, etc. Each and every one was regarded as a fresh imposition and needless waste of time.

The Queen shouldered her responsibilities with admirable patience. She was instructed in all the liturgical aspects of the ceremony and undoubtedly regarded her coronation as a religious sacrament. The fine detail of the planning staggered me. Months before the Coronation, Mike was able to tell me the exact time that St. Edward's

Crown would be placed on the Queen's head and when it would be replaced by the lighter and more comfortable Imperial State Crown for the journey back to the palace – 'Norfolk predicts it will be at 12.34, give or take a few seconds,' he said one night in an offhand aside that carried the conviction of certainty. And so it turned out.

The Earl Marshal had a reputation for being a rather unimaginative man. He took as his bible the bound copy of the plans drawn up for the Coronation of King George VI in 1937. It was amusing to hear from Mike some of the things that had gone wrong then, such as the crown nearly being placed on the King's head the wrong way round. To avoid the same mistake being made for his daughter, two studs were fixed to mark the front of the crown. Also, the lace on the cushions bearing the regalia had got caught in the medals of those carrying them so, as a precaution this time round, all the trimmings were removed.

Initially, it had also been decided that the Coronation should not be televised. Sir Winston Churchill and the Archbishop of Canterbury, among others, felt strongly that the presence of cameras would reduce the event to a glorified 'peep show'. The Coronation Commission agreed but when a resolution was put to Parliament eighty MPs voiced their disapproval and the decision was reversed, with far-reaching results. In 1952, television was still a novelty; there were barely a-million-and-a-half television sets in the whole country. When it became known that the Coronation was going to be televised, that figure doubled in a matter of months and didn't stop rising, year after year, for decades. After the Coronation, British hearths and homes would never be the same again.

Day by day, on the large scale and in detail, the jigsaw pieces were falling into place. A canvas town was set up in Kensington Gardens as temporary barracks for the hundreds of troops arriving from all corners of the Commonwealth. The Maids of Honour were instructed to provide themselves with crushable vials of smelling salts in case of fainting. And as an extra precaution twenty-five doctors were assigned for duty at Westminster Abbey on the day itself.

Another problem was the shortage of both horses and carriages. The Queen, with her well-known love for horses, particularly wanted to see them well represented in the pageantry. In order to meet the requirements seven carriages had to be retrieved from a film company who had acquired them during an austerity auction. Horses were borrowed from those London breweries still using drays for delivering beer.

An annex was added to the Abbey, in a bold modernist style, all glass and curves. Ten gorgeously sculpted fantasy creatures, modeled on the Kynge's Beastes of Hampton Court, were placed inside. It fell to the Queen's dresser, Bobo MacDonald, to notice – with the Coronation only three days away – that the one truly crucial item had been overlooked: there was not a single mirror to be seen anywhere.

The excitement aroused by the coming Coronation was temporarily dampened by the death, in March 1953, of the Queen's grandmother, Queen Mary. She had less of the natural charm that made her daughter-in-law, the Queen Mother, so attractive. To me, Queen Mary presented a sad figure, burdened by a longevity that saw one of her sons abdicate while another two died before her. She was a symbolic survivor from the old days of imperial grandeur, unsure and somewhat disapproving of the manner in which she was swept along in the ever-changing 20th Century. She abhorred the telephone, for example, and would never willingly hold the receiver.

After the death of King George V, Queen Mary lived alone in Marlborough House, keeping her own counsel but being regularly visited by her dutiful family. She was devoted to needlework, a passion she passed on to her sons. All of them when young had learned to crochet and continued to do so, to keep their hands busy whenever they sought to relax or contemplate. Queen Mary herself spent eight years embroidering a single carpet that was auctioned off for charity and eventually shipped to Canada.

She was also very fond of tennis, especially at Wimbledon, a passion I shared. Every moment I could spare during Wimbledon fortnight was spent there. As a rule, I was fortunate enough to get a seat in the Royal box and invariably Queen Mary would be a fellow spectator, often first to arrive and last to leave. She always brought a tin of boiled sweets which would be passed surreptitiously from person to person, well below eye-level of the other spectators.

Lyons provided the catering in those days (strawberry cream teas and chocolate cake) in a tiny room behind the Royal box, into which we would discreetly file, one by one, led by Queen Mary. She knew exactly the strengths and frailties in each player's game. I can recall the emotional scenes that greeted some of the famous victories we witnessed – most memorably the day Doris Hart, who had overcome childhood paralysis, won *three* titles. Beneath that controlled, regal exterior Queen Mary could be a very emotional person.

My own favourite Wimbledon story concerns the young athlete, Roger Bannister, who came into the Royal Box one day and sat down next to me. Just a few weeks before, Roger had run himself into History with the world's first ever four-minute mile. We chatted during tea and when the match was over he offered me a lift back to London in his old Morris Minor.

Roger tried to start the car but nothing happened. By this stage, he had been recognised and a large crowd of tennis fans had gathered round us, giggling and asking for his autograph. Roger obliged, but only signed in exchange for a push. After half a dozen signatures or so, we had enough power behind us to jump start the engine and roared through the gates in an acrid cloud of exhaust fumes.

All went well as far as Battersea Bridge, when the little car developed a wheeze, followed by a cough and then had a complete seizure. Roger got out to investigate. He disappeared under the bonnet and re-surfaced some ten minutes later with oil and grease all over his face and hands. The car did start by some miracle, but how we got home I'll never know – 'I don't know why I bother,' sighed Roger, as he dropped me at my corner – 'I could run to most places quicker than this gets me there.'

* * *

After the respectful lull occasioned by the death of Queen Mary, work on the Coronation resumed with ever greater intensity. The Whitsun holiday weekend fell a week before the Coronation and an advance guard of spectators swelled into London to get there early. On that Saturday afternoon the pavements were impassable. Shoppers jostled with sightseers until they blocked the traffic.

By this stage, most of the buildings were draped with flags and bunting. Regent Street was a-bloom with roses and the entrance to Bond Street was a triumphal arch of raised cornets. A week before the event, all traffic was banned from the whole Westminster area so that grandstands could be raised and three soaring arches erected over the Mall. Loyal subjects were arriving from all round the world. Those unable to obtain a bed or a sofa slept on park benches.

People with strategically situated balconies, some of whom I knew, were letting them for extraordinary fees, inclusive of champagne. Seats in the stands were selling for up to £100, a great deal of money in those days.

Everybody wanted a ticket for the actual ceremony. Mike was inundated by letters from people all asking the same favour – a ticket at any price. But even if he had wanted to help, he couldn't. There just wasn't enough room in the Abbey. Even the peers of the House of Lords weren't guaranteed places to see their liege-lord crowned; they had to take part in a lottery. The barons and earls who lost out lent their robes to those viscounts and marquises who'd won. So Mike could not possibly help with seats in the Abbey, although – being Mike – he did find some seats for a few close friends in the stands along the route.

By midnight on the evening of June 1st, the whole of London was a-swarm with Coronation fever. Despite the pouring rain, the streets of the West End were packed by throngs of people. It took Mike and me over an hour by car to travel the two miles from Launceston Place to the Savoy Hotel for dinner. After that, we all went to Boy Browning's flat in Chelsea with the teenage naval cadet who would be acting as Prince Philip's page in the Coronation, who was staying with us.

Well in advance of the great day I had to make my personal plans, including arranging for the children to be taken with their nanny to Buckingham Palace where they were to be the guests of Prince Charles. For weeks they had been bubbling with excitement. Everyone invited to the ceremony in the Abbey was sent a programme, listing the order of ceremony and setting out the words of the congregational responses. There was a further list prescribing what to wear.

Each person was allotted eighteen inches of seating space – the maximum available in order to accommodate over 7,000 people inside the Abbey. The women were warned not to wear furs, but were permitted a choice in dress length – long or short. Had I chosen to go short, I would have had to buy a hat to go with it, so, as I rather mistrust hats of any sort, I was only too happy to choose a long dress – with no regrets.

Hardy Amies was then the rising star of British couture and one day I went along to his Savile Row showrooms to see his collection. I was ushered into his little den where he first showed me illustrations of the basic designs. Then he called in some of his models to show off those designs which had appealed to me most. I fell in love with one and timidly asked the price, fearing that to do so was a virtual admission that I could not afford it.

'For you, Mrs. Parker, I'll do it for fifty pounds.'

Fifty pounds! An enormous sum for one dress but from him, a bargain. And such a heavenly, beautiful dress. After all, a Coronation usually happens but once in a lifetime. I selected as my fabric an exquisite shell pink duchesse satin.

The bodice had a halter neckline with shell-shaped edging. The skirt was full, with a stiffened petticoat carefully measured to be within the allotted width. Regulations decreed that the top of one's arms had to be covered and I therefore ordered a small matching bolero, a wise decision as it turned out because on the day it was freezing cold.

Once outside on the Savile Row pavement I felt stunned. In my entire life I had never spent £50 on a single item of clothing. Maybe that's why it became my favourite. I wore it a number of times at Government House on the subsequent tour of Australia. I still have it, even though I outgrew it years ago. How I wish my waist was still 23 inches! Whenever I give my wardrobe a spring-clean, my Coronation dress always escapes the dustbin because of the memories attached.

* * *

It was arranged for Phyllis Horsley and me to attend the Coronation ceremony together. Mike was right at the back of the congregation near the door and only saw the ceremony on the television monitors nearby. Phyllis and I had seats in the gallery above the peeresses, with a commanding view. We had to be in our places by 7.00 a.m. In fact, most of the congregation were in their places long before the Queen finished her breakfast.

Mike too was on duty early. He woke at dawn to a

more confused morning scramble than normal because, like many Londoners, we had our own Coronation house guest to look after, a Royal Navy cadet called Nigel Rees who'd been selected by Prince Philip to be his page. Nigel had been head of the passing out parade at the Officer Cadet Training Centre, *H.M.S. Devonshire*. Prince Philip had noticed him during the inspection and, impressed with his bearing, asked him on the spot to do the job. It wasn't an entirely random decision, however, as Prince Philip himself had won the King's Dirk at Dartmouth for being top cadet in his term. It was left to Mike, of course, to sort out the details.

Mike and Nigel whizzed off to Buckingham Palace in one car. I left in another car half an hour later and headed for Boy Browning's flat in Chelsea. Left behind were Nanny, Julie and Michael waiting for yet a third car to collect them for the day at Buckingham Palace.

The weather was wet and cold. The downpour that had begun the previous evening continued unremittingly as if to mock the choice of date, June 2nd being on record as being the most consistently sunny day in the British calendar. Phyllis and I shivered in our seats, high up among the scaffolding that hung like grotesque cobwebs all around the Abbey. Behind us, we could hear the raindrops pinging off the galvanised roofs of the portable lavatories.

Knowing in advance how long we would have to wait before the ceremony, we had all come prepared with something to eat. I saw duchesses nibbling hardboiled eggs and baronesses with dainty, stamp-sized sandwiches. Most of the menfolk seemed to have hip-flasks. I had one myself, filled with fortifying brandy. Also tucked away in my bag was a small tube of Horlicks tablets, a handkerchief, my make-up and the essential safety pin. On the way back from having a nip of brandy in the lavatory I noticed that an exclusive litter of Fortnum and Mason wrappings was gathering under the scaffolding like a drift of autumn leaves. The only excitement, while the congregation waited in the cold, was provided by a man on the end of our row who nearly fell off his seat onto the peeresses below.

By eight o'clock the peers of the realm and the military top brass and their wives were in place. By nine, the European cousins of the Royal Family had joined them. At nine-thirty a buffet breakfast was served in the annex. By now we realised that the procession must be on its way. The Queen and Prince Philip were due to leave Buckingham Palace soon after ten o'clock in the gold State Coach.

This latter arrangement had been the subject of perplexed debate. Mike had told me there was no real precedent for a reigning Queen going to her Coronation together with her Consort so the question had arisen – what about Prince Philip? Should he follow the Queen on horseback? Or in a separate coach? Or what?

Commonsense prevailed and Prince Philip went in the same coach as his wife, keeping in touch with the palace through a radio telephone on the seat beside him. Wherever he went, he maintained contact with the office and all his cars, including the one he had given to us, were equipped with radio telephones.

By the time the Queen left Buckingham Palace the noise of the crowds and the music of the massed bands had almost drowned out the rain. As it grew in volume, we realised that the Queen was nearing the Abbey. Four women attendants appeared to brush the floor around St. Edward's chair. Then the choir ceased singing. The Queen had by now entered the Abbey and was being enrobed for the ceremony.

A hush fell over all. Just the sound of the rain.

Then, quite suddenly, from the boys of Westminster School – 'Vivat Regina! Vivat Regina Elizabeth! Vivat! Vivat! Vivat' – and at that moment the Queen made her entrance, from which point on she was on her own.

For two and a half hours the Queen was the sole focus of attention, not only of all those assembled in the Abbey but of millions around the world who were able to receive the television transmission. Everyone present was aware of the tremendous strain the Queen was under, facing such an ordeal at the age of twenty-seven.

After a brief pause for a moment of private prayer, the Queen took up her position in front of St. Edward's chair. The regalia was passed to the altar and the Archbishop of Canterbury showed the Queen in turn to the four points of the compass – 'Sirs, I here present unto you Queen Elizabeth, your undoubted Queen, wherefore all you who are come this day to do your homage and service, are you willing to do the same?'

'God save Queen Elizabeth!' we responded in unison.

The ceremony then progressed through a sacramental phase, leading up to the placing of the crown on the Queen's head. At this moment I saw Prince Charles escorted to the Queen Mother's side dressed in a white satin suit. As Duke of Cornwall he was the senior Royal Duke and consequently Head of the Peerage and entitled to lead the obeisance though, yet again, there was no precedent for one so young.

The anointing took place under a canopy supported by four Knights of the Garter. The television cameras were turned away from the scene, and I was too far away to hear the responses. I glanced down at Prince Charles and saw him wipe his head with his hand and then smell it. Later, I learned from Mike that Nurse Lightbody had that morning put pomade on his hair to keep it in place and he wasn't used to it.

The Dean of Westminster solemnly carried the crown from the Altar on a cushion to the Archbishop and paused. One could hear the muted scraping as the peerage reached for their coronets and caps which had been tucked under their seats. The Archbishop raised the crown high in the sight of the people then placed it gently on the Queen's head. With a slight movement of her hand, she steadied it.

Immediately after the peers had put their coronets on, there was an almighty shout – 'GOD SAVE THE QUEEN!!' and a fanfare blazed out. The bells began to peal and at this signal the artillery at the Tower of London fired their twenty-one-gun salute. The crowd outside roared and cheered. After the stillness of the religious rites the sudden volley of sound had a shattering force to it. Prince Philip knelt at his wife's feet – 'I, Philip, Duke of Edinburgh, do become your liege man of life and limb, and of earthly worship; and faith and truth I will bear unto you, to live and die, against all manner of folks. So help me God.'

There he was, that confident, self-assured young officer I had come to know so many years before – leading the nation in homage. As he rose, Prince Philip touched the crown and kissed the Queen's left cheek. The crown wobbled just slightly and once more the Queen had to steady it before the other Royal Dukes assumed the stage. All the ranks of peerage were represented by oath-swearers until the Coronation was completed. Then the Queen proceeded through St. Edward's Chapel and out of sight.

* * *

Mike and I, in the company of Nigel Rees, left the Abbey by boat from Westminster Pier and then by a palace car to Launceston Place. I had not been able to catch any kind of glimpse of the procession so the first thing I did was to turn on the television set. When Julie and Michael came home much later, Julie burst excitedly into the room with the wide eyes of one who'd been dazzled, while Michael seemed just as impressed with the simultaneous news that Mount Everest had been conquered at last by the climbers Edmund Hilary and Tenzing Norgay.

Later that evening, when the children were tucked in bed, Mike and I attended a Coronation Ball at the Savoy Hotel. Cecil Beaton provided the decoration and Sir Winston and Lady Churchill were among the guests. When Sir Winston made his entrance on the arm of his old friend, the Pasha of Marrakesh, Lord of the Atlas, all the other guests burst into spontaneous applause. By midnight we were all in high spirits, perhaps because of the firework displays that went on until the early hours of the morning but more likely because of the all champagne we'd had – over three thousand bottles between us.

Looking back at that day, the Coronation remains in my memory as the most inspiring royal event I ever saw. Decades later I still find it hard to convince myself that something mystical did not occur. I have a recording of the music played during the service and whenever I listen to *Zadok the Priest*, I re-experience a tremor of excitement.

Afterwards, to help defray the cost of the ceremony, most of the furnishings used were sold off. Guests were entitled to purchase their seats for £7, each one of them individually numbered (Mike's and mine were numbered 41 and 3). Five tons of specially woven Axminster carpet were cut into strips and sold at auction. On a more bizarre note, among the rubbish sifted through afterwards was an emerald necklace. More than a month went by before its owner realised it was missing and came forward to claim it.

* * *

Eight days after the Coronation, it was Prince Philip's 32nd birthday and Mike threw a party in his honour at Launceston Place. Prince Philip's sisters had remained in England to enjoy the post-Coronation festivities and they too were invited. Margarita and Theodora ('Dolla') were both rather stoutly built, whereas Sophie, the youngest, was tall and slender. All three thoroughly enjoyed being with their younger brother in informal surroundings away from the more official atmosphere of Buckingham Palace and they chatted freely all evening, sometimes speaking in German for their more private comments among themselves.

Princess Sophie, who spoke fairly fluent English, asked at one point if she could go up and see Julie in bed. With all the noise and excitement going on downstairs, I knew she would still be awake and took the Princess upstairs. Sophie sat down on the edge of the bed and started to read Julie a story. After a few minutes I began to fret about my duties as hostess – 'Don't worry,' said Sophie, pushing me gently toward the door – 'You go. I'll stay here.'

As I descended the stairs, I smiled to myself at hearing the familiar words of *Little Red Riding Hood* floating through the bedroom door in a guttural German accent.

When I rejoined the party I found Mike and Boy mixing cocktails from a crate of Australian champagne while Prince Philip was explaining to Prince Alfonso Hohenlohe how the glass-blower had managed to trap a bubble of air in the stem of his champagne glass. Prince Alfonso was a frequent visitor to Launceston Place, before and after the Coronation. He would often dine with us or invite us to his restaurant in London. One night when he and Mike were playing squash, the Prince tumbled and broke his arm. Mike whisked him off to the casualty department of St. George's Hospital – 'I am Mike Parker, Prince Philip's Private Secretary, and this is Prince Alfonso Hohenlohe. He's broken his arm. Can you fix him up quick?'

The porter looked up wearily – 'All right, sir. Just take a seat over there between Horatio Nelson and the Queen of Sheba.'

Mike rarely tried to pull rank but he knew how to deal with sarcasm. As a result Alfonso did get speedy attention and was soon X-rayed and bandaged up. He was certainly fully healed in time for our summer holidays when Mike flew us out to the Prince's new beach resort which he had opened at a sleepy Spanish fishing village called Marbella. Peter Horsley and Phyllis, together with Mike and myself, were among the very first guests at what became The Marbella Club. Alfonso was known in the British newspapers as a playboy, but he had a good head for business and Mike had given him support and encouragement from the start. To

201

honour our arrival, Alfonso nailed a Royal Navy crest above the doorway of our cabin and an R.A.F. crest over the Horsleys'.

It was one of those rare and wonderful holidays where everything was perfect. The sun blazed down from a cloudless sky, the service was faultless and the company in the evenings entertaining. We explored the coast and countryside by car and boat and made a quick foray to Gibraltar to pay a courtesy call on the Governor. I'll never forget the looks we received, entering Government House looking like beachcombers.

* * *

Chapter 14

Princess Margaret and Peter Townsend

As Princess Margaret was leaving Westminster Abbey after the Coronation, she paused and reached up to brush a speck of dust from Peter Townsend's shoulder. It was a simple womanly gesture but the fact that it occurred so naturally and spontaneously alerted every reporter who saw it. Rumours that the Princess and her equerry were in love had been swirling around for months and here was apparent confirmation. In public. On camera. It *must* be love. What else could it mean?

The next day in New York, the Princess Margaret-Peter Townsend angle featured prominently in the newspapers' Coronation coverage. The Americans were far less deferential in the way they treated the Royal Family, especially Princess Margaret who looked like a celebrity and behaved like one. Speculation about her romantic life had become a staple topic in the gossip columns and women's magazines since Peter Townsend's divorce, a few months previously. His future intentions, as seen from New York, were therefore considered to be fair game.

On the British side of the Atlantic, different rules applied. Every newspaper loves a scandal but tittle-tattle written up for American readers had to be taken far more seriously by British editors. The prestige of the monarchy, before and after the Queen's coronation, had never been higher and the press had played its part by jumping on the band-wagon early and banging the drum the loudest. Everybody knew that something was going on between the Princess and her equerry but few people outside Buckingham Palace were quite sure how serious their 'friendship' was. So Fleet Street's editors decided to sit on the story in the hope that someone quotable might say something for them to report. Buckingham Palace said nothing.

It goes against nature to expect Fleet Street's finest to look the other way while their American rivals are having fun with a juicy scandal involving the British Royal Family. Ten days after the Coronation, one London tabloid, *The Sunday People*, broke ranks – 'Stop These Scandalous Rumours'.

It was a classic newspaper ploy. By condemning the rumours *The Sunday People* was challenging Buckingham Palace to come clean and make a statement one way or the other. Was Princess Margaret in love with her equerry or not?

The normal reaction inside Buckingham Palace would

have been to follow the long-standing and often effective precedent of dealing with the press: ignore them and they might go away. This was different. This time, the Household was involved at a personal level. Some senior courtiers really did disapprove of what was going on between Princess Margaret and Peter Townsend, of whom they'd been wary from the start, first as an outsider and later with a degree of jealousy as they observed his growing influence with the King and Queen and Princess Margaret.

Any prospect of a morganatic marriage between a royal Princess and a mere equerry was intolerable to the men whose inherited mission in life was to preserve and protect the pre-eminence of the Crown. But that was not the only issue. In 1953, Peter Townsend was nearly forty years of age. Despite his youthful good looks, he was a middle-aged man with two children. Princess Margaret was nearly half his age and sister of the Queen, the Head of the Church of England, who had just sworn before a global audience of millions to uphold its precepts as Defender of the Faith. That's why the relationship between Peter Townsend and Princess Margaret was scandalous in the eyes of the Church – he was divorced. June, 1953 was a very inconvenient time to have a couple of love-struck home-wreckers on the premises.

* * *

Princess Margaret was a seventeen-year-old schoolgirl when I first met her and even then she knew her own mind. At her best, she was a sweet, impetuous young woman with all the charm of vivacious youth. At her worst, she could display a perverse sense of naughtiness. Her character was well captured by her former governess, a Scottish woman called Marion Crawford, who in 1950 published an account of her experiences in *The Little Princesses*. Mostly, this book was totally harmless. It revealed, for example, that the Princesses subscribed to the *Children's Newspaper*, wrote nice thank you letters after Christmas and birthdays and were fond of an occasional trip to the pantomime.

Hereafter, Crawfie, as she was nicknamed by the Princesses, took to full-time journalism. *Crawfie's Column*, her regular round-up of royal comings and goings, was syndicated in women's magazines around the world. Her disclosures, such as they were, lost her the affection of the Royal Family and the respect of the entire Household. It was thanks to Crawfie's perceived betrayal of trust that Household staff were henceforward required to sign a declaration of confidentiality as a condition of employment. Even Mike had to sign one.

Crawfie's career as a chronicler of royal events came to an end when she reported with a wealth of purple prose on Royal Ascot and Trooping the Colour not knowing that the first of them had been postponed and the second one cancelled. In her book about the Princesses, however, writing from personal experience, she presented an accurate double portrait recognisable to everyone in the Household.

To put it in a nutshell, from adolescence onward, Princess Elizabeth had been taken in hand and trained for her destiny as heir to the throne whereas Princess Margaret ... well, what was her role to be? There was no obvious answer. When Princess Elizabeth fell in love with a dashing young naval officer, Princess Margaret was still taking music lessons. From what I was given to understand afterwards, King George found it difficult to accept that his Lilibet had fallen in love with almost the first determined suitor she'd met. The King would have preferred her to wait before marrying, as he had waited for Elizabeth Bowes-Lyon, bringing happiness to them both. Did the King feel he had 'lost' his elder daughter too soon – to her duty, if not to another man? Was that why the King devoted so much attention to Princess Margaret, materially and emotionally – to compensate her for being over-shadowed by her sister?

Many times at Buckingham Palace I noticed how, when Princess Margaret and her father were together, he would openly admire and compliment her. It was clear for all to see that he doted on her. All she had to do was to give him a spontaneous hug of affection to bring a glow of pleasure to his face – 'I know I shouldn't spoil her,' he would say, almost apologetically, 'but I can't help it.'

Princess Margaret was showered with gifts by her indulgent parents. I remember once coming down in the

Palace lift with the Princess, Mike and Prince Philip. We were going to a party at the Dorchester.

'Do you like my new necklace?' she asked, arching her throat to display a string of pearls the size of peas.

'Yes, they're divine,' I replied.

'I think so, too,' she said rather smugly. 'Mummy gave them to me tonight. I honestly don't know what came over her.'

Prince Philip turned to Mike and me with raised eyebrows.

Princess Margaret was well accustomed to getting her own way. When the 'New Look' came into fashion, she was one of the first to flaunt her wedge heels, ankle socks, and long, wide skirts. When Queen Mary voiced disapproval of Princess Margaret smoking in public, she responded by being photographed with longer and more outrageous cigarette holders.

Another incident neatly sums up Prince Philip's attitude to the 'Margaret Phenomenon'. It happened at the annual Diplomatic Corps reception in November of 1951, the last one that King George was well enough to attend. Prince Philip, Mike and I were chatting in a Palace corridor, when a footman passed by carrying a hat box. He was in such a hurry he was almost running. Prince Philip stopped him and asked him why the rush? The footman replied he was carrying Princess Margaret's tiara.

'Oh, yes,' commented Prince Philip wryly. 'It's the first time Margaret's ever worn one in public and she's very excited about it.'

Princess Margaret in those days was highly susceptible to some of the teasing she had to endure from Prince Philip, sometimes unjustly. But she could be charming when she wished. Another time, I was passing the open door to her room when she came out and sweetly begged me to fasten her necklace. I had no idea where her dresser, Ruby – Bobo MacDonald's sister – was, but I happily obliged. It was made of exquisite diamonds. She confided to me they had been a present from Field Marshal Smuts during the tour of South Africa.

Princess Elizabeth always commanded a consistent level of formality. Even in private I never addressed her as anything other than 'Mam' and Prince Philip as 'Sir'. Between ourselves, Mike and I referred to him as 'P.P.' never as 'Philip'. Princess Margaret, on the other hand, didn't know from one week to the next whether she wanted to be treated as the Little Princess or Cinderella. Often she appeared to wish to be a combination of both.

On a trip to the Palladium, to see the American comedian and singer, Danny Kaye, Princess Margaret wasn't content just to see the show from the best seats; she wanted to meet him personally. So afterwards all of us trooped down to see Danny in his dressing-room. Princess Margaret was a dedicated fan, and knew the words of many of his songs. Sometimes, she would invent words of her own and turn them into lampoons of Household characters. Now, she bounced up and down excitedly demanding a reprise of one of Danny Kaye's most popular numbers – 'Do *Ballin' the Jack*, Danny! Oh please, do *Ballin' the Jack*.'

Danny Kaye responded to her enthusiasm with good humour. He had brought a Polaroid camera with him from America, the first I had ever seen. Danny showed us how it worked to produce instant photos whereupon, amid shared hilarity, we all struck poses for a group portrait.

* * *

By the time Princess Margaret reached twenty-one years of age, she was at the centre of her own social clique known to gossip columnists as 'the Margaret Set'. They were written up as being rather raffish and wild, in the sense that they drank cocktails in night clubs and stayed up late dancing. These days, such behaviour is considered a normal rite of passage. At the time, worries about Princess Margaret's friends simply added an extra headache to a Household already deeply concerned about her relationship with Peter Townsend. In their eyes, Princess Margaret was in danger of testing to destruction the rules of tolerable behaviour.

Surrounded by protocol and under constant attention in public, members of the Royal Family are necessarily restricted in their choice of personal friends. Even in private, their behaviour comes under scrutiny – from within the Household. Probably only about a dozen people are close enough to the Queen and Prince Philip to address them by their given names. For as long as Mike was at the Palace, the most faithful of the dependables were Sir Harold Wernher and his wife Lady Zia. I can hardly recall attending a function at Buckingham Palace without them being somewhere about. Lady Zia, short for Anastasia, was the daughter of Grand Duke Michael of Russia. Sir Harold's family wealth came from South African diamonds; he ran a stable of race horses as a hobby. Prince Philip and Princess Elizabeth, even after she became Queen, were often weekend guests at Luton Hoo, the Wernhers' country home in Bedfordshire, where Princess Margaret would also be invited.

Princess Margaret loved anything to do with show business and the theatre. She adored making a splash at masques and fancy dress parties. One night, soon after Princess Elizabeth and Prince Philip moved into Clarence House, I was taken by surprise when Mike came home early to change for a fancy dress party and fetched his dinner jacket from the wardrobe.

'I thought it was fancy dress?' I said.

'It is,' he replied.

'So what are you going as?'

'You'll see,' was all he would say, keeping me in suspense.

The following morning I discovered the mystery. The party had been held at the American Ambassador's house with his daughter, Sharman, acting as hostess. She was an ambitious young lady determined to break into the highest-toned circles, which is why she had invited Princess Margaret and other members of the Royal Family.

Prince Philip, Princess Elizabeth and Mike went to the Sharmans' *soiree* as the three characters in Bing Crosby's hit of the day, *The Waiter, the Porter and the Upstairs Maid*. They made their entrance singing that song to a mimed tableau of their own improvisation, which must have made quite an impression because they won first prize. Princess Margaret upstaged them however by appearing in a can-can outfit as 'Madame Fifi', complete with lace panties, black stockings and suspenders. She finished in true Parisian fashion by hoisting her petticoats and wiggling her *derriere* in a finale that brought wolf-whistles and loud applause from an appreciative audience. Wherever she went the Princess attracted handsome men, but the only one she loved was Peter Townsend.

* * *

To start with, when Peter first arrived at Buckingham Palace as a temporary equerry, he was supposed to alternate his Palace duties with work in the R.A.F. but, as with Mike and Prince Philip, it soon became impossible to tell whether he was 'on' duty or 'off'. I had not been to the Palace more than half-a-dozen times when I felt impelled to ask Mike if the gossip in the corridors – about Peter and Princess Margaret – was true. Why was Peter Townsend always around?

'Isn't it obvious?' was his laconic reply. 'Of course there's something going on.'

A few months later Mike and I were strolling in Windsor Great Park while waiting for him to go in for his innings during a cricket match. Suddenly, there was the sound of high-spirited horses cantering ahead of us and within seconds Princess Margaret and Peter appeared, playing a game of mounted tag. They both pulled their horses up sharply when they saw us. Not only were they surprised but visibly embarrassed. We exchanged greetings, followed swiftly by 'Goodbye' as the horses were spurred back into the chase.

Rosemary Townsend and I were both married to men lured from us by the allure of glittering prizes. But at least, to the very best of my knowledge, Mike was not having an affair. Rosemary, as a wife and mother, had to stand to one side while Princess Margaret, hardly out of ankle socks, entertained her husband. Understandably, she had every cause to sound bitter sometimes. One night, when I was still a comparatively new Household wife, Rosemary and I sat next to each other at a reception. During the conversation Rosemary asked me how I was enjoying life.

'It has its moments,' I answered.

Rosemary gave me a pitying look.

'You wait,' she said. 'There's a lot more in store for you yet. Where is Mike? I haven't seen him all evening.'

Rosemary Townsend spent most of her days isolated

in Adelaide Cottage, on the Windsor estate, a place she disliked intensely, describing it as the dampest and coldest house in England. It was prey to river mists and in winter she sometimes felt so cold she had to wear a coat indoors. It was here she stayed with her two sons for company while her husband spent most of his weeks in London.

Peter lost a great deal of respect over the way he handled his divorce from Rosemary, who in her frustration became involved with another man. Despite the fact that all in the Household were fully aware of what was going on, Townsend reacted to Rosemary's affair with the righteous indignation of a man betrayed. He sued for divorce on the uncontested grounds of adultery and by the beginning of 1953 he was a free man again – Deputy Master of the Household at Clarence House and spending most of his days there with the Queen Mother and Princess Margaret.

* * *

It was the Townsends' divorce, six months before the Coronation, that first put the Peter-Margaret problem into the public domain. The first obstacle had been overcome in so far as Peter's divorce freed him to marry again. The second obstacle was more complicated. In order to marry, Princess Margaret and Peter needed the new Queen's approval. She knew about the romance but with the Coronation to consider, domestic matters had had to be put on one side.

The Queen's Press Secretary, Richard Colville (Harrow, Royal Navy) was one of the old guard of courtiers inherited from her father. He didn't really like news or the people who made it, preferring much of the time to keep the press at bay with a taciturn 'no comment'. That worked for a while but only until that moment, on the steps of Westminster Abbey, when Princess Margaret oh-so-naturally turned to her lover to brush a smut from his lapel and signaled to the world how close they really were.

Knowing Princess Margaret to be a strong-willed young woman, I fully expected her to marry Peter, if for no other reason than to show that she could. Mike was better informed and told me that, apart from the Church of England frowning upon the re-marriage of divorced people, there were also constitutional barriers. No member of the Royal Family was permitted to marry before the age of twenty-five without the consent of the Sovereign; and even then Princess Margaret would have to give the Privy Council a year's notice of her intentions. Both Houses of Parliament would also have to approve her choice of spouse.

The newspapers, having been reluctant to get involved in the story too soon, were now even more reluctant to let go. As news, it was an irresistible mix of royalty and true love, guaranteed to keep readers engaged. Every new rumour or hopeful piece of speculation was met with silence from Buckingham Palace. Nobody, apparently, wanted Princess Margaret to marry the man of her choice. The Household was against it. Sir Winston Churchill was against it. The Church was against it. Prince Philip was against it. The Queen was torn between what she realised must be her duty and loyalty to her younger sister.

The Peter-Margaret affair was spinning out of control as the whole country took sides. How far, as a nation, were we entitled to interfere in the private lives of our Royal Family? Did it not seem preposterous that a modern woman of twenty-three could not marry the man she loved purely because of an accident of birth? Wasn't the Church of England's attitude to divorce out of date? The Prime Minister-designate, Anthony Eden, was a divorced person as were various members of the cabinet and members of both Houses of Parliament – was it fair for a Royal marriage to be vetoed because of a law passed some two hundred years ago?

A breathing space was required for the whole issue to be considered in a calmer atmosphere. Princess Margaret rejected point-blank any suggestion that she should end her relationship with Peter Townsend, the man who had been by her side for years and who had consoled her during the traumatic bereavement of the King's death. However, she did allow herself to be persuaded that a temporary separation would do no harm.

Thus, at the end of June 1953, in the lull following the Coronation and as press speculation continued, Princess Margaret departed with her mother for a tour of Rhodesia. The day before her return to London, Peter Townsend was flown out to take up a new posting for one year as an attaché at the British Embassy in Brussels. I learned from the Household of Princess Margaret's deep disappointment and even anger at the way things had been arranged – behind her back, as she saw it. At any rate, a showdown had been postponed, if only temporarily.

* * *

Chapter 15

Prince Philip's Mother

The comings and goings of Buckingham Palace had become so much a part of my life by the time of the Coronation that I could hardly be compared to the young wife and mother who'd felt so awestruck at the Queen's wedding in 1947. I was used to entertaining all sorts at Launceston Place. One of the Royal relations whom I grew to like very much was Princess Margarita of Baden, a tall, well-built blonde girl with blue eyes. She was a niece of Prince Philip's training as a nurse at St. Thomas's Hospital. She felt quite lonely in London and, having met me at the Palace once or twice, used to invite herself round for supper. Princess Margarita was only too glad to keep me and the children company during the long evenings when Mike was on duty.

Perhaps my favourite and very special visitor was Prince Philip's mother, Princess Alice, a lovely personality.

She would make a habit of dropping in after dinner for coffee and cigarettes, both of which she liked strong. She was an inveterate smoker, puffing away at her cigarettes as she carried on an animated conversation in a husky voice with just a hint of an accent. She would sit on our sofa within close range of an ashtray and start the conversation with a detailed progress report on her grandson, Prince Charles, whom she adored. The only time I remember her wearing anything other than her grey nun's habit was at the wedding of Princess Elizabeth and Prince Philip, when she walked down the aisle in a sweeping gown of purple and a plumed toque.

In repose her face was rather grave, which together with her erect carriage and grey habit contributed to a somewhat austere impression. But she could become very lively and was a marvellous story-teller. Although she had endured her fair share of tragedy, she never sounded remotely self-pitying. For me it was refreshing to find someone with the serene surety of God's mercy, but without any moral presumption.

Princess Alice and Lord Mountbatten were among the children of Prince Louis of Battenberg who inherited his title and estates in Hesse in Germany. Princess Alice was born sixteen years before Queen Victoria died and in her lifetime saw the enormous changes which now make that era seem centuries ago. She was born with a congenital speech defect which had caused almost total deafness by the time I got to know her. It was not until Mike mentioned it to me that I learned of her handicap, although I had noticed how she concentrated on my face whenever I spoke. At the time, I had accepted it as a family trait since Prince Philip has the same attitude in conversation and looks you straight in the eye.

Princess Alice learnt to lip-read in English, Greek, French and German. It was interesting to observe how close she and Prince Philip were to each other because they had a way of communicating by simple gesture. Similarly, incidentally, King George and his daughter Princess Elizabeth could communicate with each other by merely raising an eyebrow. Deafness invariably lends a certain remoteness to its sufferers. They often feel cut off from the outside world and there are other disadvantages. When Princess Alice married according to the Greek Orthodox rite she was unable to read the priests' lips through their thick, bushy beards and so, when they asked if she had been betrothed to anyone else, she said 'yes' – and when they asked if she was marrying of her own free will – 'no'.

Her husband, Prince Andrew, was a career soldier, not exactly a safe profession for a Greek prince. If he was not fighting the Turks, there was civil conflict to contend with at home. And life did not become much easier for Princess Alice when she and Prince Andrew were exiled after he had been put on trial for his life. The Prince languished without a sense of purpose and they drifted into an unhappy separation.

In 1937 their third daughter, Cecile, was killed in a plane crash. Princess Alice, seeking solace in her religion, wanted to found a new religious order, but was given no support by the Greek Orthodox Church. Instead, she involved herself in setting up an orphanage in Athens. During the Second World War, when the Germans occupied Athens, she refused any preferential treatment offered by the invaders. Her father was German and her daughters were all married to German officers but her son was in the Royal Navy. Conflicts of loyalty only seemed to deepen her religious faith – 'God had work to do and I was a pair of hands.'

The only reward she received for her sacrifices was to be sent into exile once more. By then she was a woman of sixty and a widow. Her husband had been confined on a boat in Monte Carlo harbour throughout the war and there he died in 1944. One of Prince Philip's most poignant duties on his return from the Pacific was to wind up his father's estate.

Princess Alice continued to devote her life to others and was not afraid to use what influence she had to assist the deprived and needy. The birth of Prince Charles, for example, brought a mountain of unsolicited toys to Buckingham Palace. All of these were carefully sifted through and labeled, and a fair selection parceled off to Princess Alice for distribution among her orphans in Athens. Whenever Prince Philip made a spring clean of his possessions – he was a hoarder of 'things that will come in useful' – he would always see to it that a small pile of discarded but still serviceable items would find their way to Mama.

Princess Alice lived simply and never came to England with more than one suitcase – 'I don't have enough things to fill two,' she would state calmly.

Many of her characteristics are reflected in her son, the same sense of dedication and self-discipline. She showed great pride in his character and in his achievements. He was her only son, and the youngest of her children, and there was a very special bond between them.

* * *

Chapter 16

On Tour in Australia

Reasoning with my heart and not my head, I sighed with relief when the Coronation was over – hoping that Mike and I might get the chance to see each other more often. I had not taken into account the ensuing royal tours. In June, shortly after she was crowned, the Queen paid a Coronation visit to Scotland, followed in July by one to Wales, followed in turn by visits all over England. In addition to all this, Mike had to squeeze in preparations for a very extensive tour of the Commonwealth, which involved revising the programme set up for the tour that was cancelled on the death of the King.

When Mike was not on duty at official events, he would spend late evenings at the office working on his plans. Every time-zone around the world had to be checked, every minute calculated. The sad point had arrived in our marriage when Mike and I were talking to each other on the telephone more often than face to face. All the discontents in our lives clashed. We had reached the stage where we were going in different directions.

Mike made it quite plain, by his words and his actions, that his career at the side of Prince Philip and Queen Elizabeth was far more important than his family responsibilities. He was even too busy, when the time came, to find a school for his son. In the end, I turned to Boy Browning for advice. He helpfully used his influence to get Michael into West Downs Preparatory School, taking me down one afternoon to meet the headmaster.

Later, when Michael reached the age for public school, Mike did take an interest – he definitely wanted his son to go to Prince Philip's old school, Gordonstoun. It would have proved no problem getting him in but Mike should have realised that Michael didn't have the temperament for the harsh Gordonstoun curriculum. Michael was shy, not particularly assertive, a typical late developer. When I told Boy Browning of Mike's intentions he sided with me.

Gordonstoun was the brainchild of Kurt Hahn, who had previously run a school at Salem, in Germany, which emphasised character building rather than book learning. Prince Philip was taught there until, with the rise of Hitler, Hahn left for Scotland, feeling he had no place in any Nazi Third Reich. Morayshire provided a much more congenial setting and soon Prince Philip was re-united with his former mentor.

Apart from Uncle Dickie, Kurt Hahn was the next most formative male influence on Prince Philip's adult character, as he readily admits. There's no doubt that Hahn's gift for drawing out the best in people found a responsive chord in the young Greek-British prince. The secret in getting the best out of boys, said Hahn, is to make them feel wanted and Prince Philip thrived on the Gordonstoun regime. He was made Guardian, or head boy, and Mike decided that what was good enough for Prince Philip was good enough for Michael. When I protested, he shushed me – 'Stop worrying, it'll knock the spots off the lad.'

It took all my resourcefulness to talk him out of sending Michael to Gordonstoun. It was already obvious that Prince Charles would receive part of his education there – what more glowing recommendation did a parent need? But Mike, because of his prolonged absences, didn't see Michael as often as I did and my intuition told me that Gordonstoun was no place for a sensitive boy like mine.

Eventually, Peter Horsley came to my rescue by suggesting his old school, Wellington College, as a possibility. Peter took me down to see the place, I liked it and put Michael on the list straight away. I hadn't told Mike I was even visiting the school. When I returned with the prospectus he was too nonplussed, at having the matter taken out of his hands, to do anything more about it.

There could be no doubt what was happening. Mike was drifting away from us. Increasingly, I would have to turn to the Palace secretaries to find out where he was and sometimes even they didn't know. Once, I had to suffer the embarrassment of Prince Philip telephoning me – 'Where's Mike' he asked when I answered.

'I don't know,' I replied. 'I thought he was with you.'

'Oh, no,' said Prince Philip, 'he's got the night off tonight.'

Then he laughed and apologised for disturbing me and hung up.

Some nights Mike didn't come home at all, with no explanations given and no thought that I might have been lying awake all night, thinking the worst. When he did come home he was usually late and when he wasn't late we were disinclined to be civil towards each other. That's when I moved into the spare room.

Yet, in the midst of all this emotional upheaval, there were still fleeting moments when Mike could make me laugh again, when I still felt my love for him despite fearing, as I did, that the impending Coronation Tour of the Commonwealth would break us apart. Those feelings must have been shared by Mike because when I beseeched him to take me to Australia, for the sake of reconciliation, he agreed. With his usual efficiency he managed to fix berths for Julie and myself on a cargo steamer that would take us to Australia in time for the Royal tour.

* * *

The official starting date for the Commonwealth Tour was November 23rd, 1953. The new Royal Yacht, *Britannia* wasn't quite ready so the Queen flew out to Bermuda to rendezvous with the old one, a converted cruise ship called *S.S. Gothic*. Julie and I, meanwhile, were already on our way to Australia. Our ship was a cargo steamer called *Wanstead*, making her maiden voyage.

We had let the house in Launceston Place for six months so Julie and I spent the eve of our intended departure at the good old De Vere Hotel. Unfortunately, the next day dawned through a thick fog and the sailing was postponed. It felt very strange to be marooned just around the corner from our own home and Julie became restless. I telephoned Mike and he suggested I come around to Buckingham Palace where Julie played most of day with the Royal children, although Charles was absent part of the time, attending lessons.

The following morning, the air was crisp and clear and there was just sufficient mist on the Thames for me to feel hopeful of the adventure – six whole weeks of blue skies and fresh sea breezes would perhaps help with the anxieties and despair clouding my feelings about the state of my marriage. I had no one to appease, no appearances to keep up, only Julie to look after, who was fast growing into a lively young lady. We played board games, read everything in print on board and each morning I gave her lessons, having brought with me full instructions from her headmistress.

As we steamed further and further away from the

British winter, and into the Indian Ocean, the *Wanstead's* crew set up a canvas swimming pool on deck and helped to teach Julie to swim. They all knew who my husband was and that we were on our way to join him. They showed nothing but courtesy and consideration for my needs and even moderated their language in my presence – a commendable but unnecessary gesture considering that I was an ex-Wren.

The only other passenger was a young doctor going out to his first practice in Australia. He joined in what became the daily highlight of our journey – feeding the animals. As cargo, the ship was carrying two racehorses, four prize bulls and two pedigree labrador dogs. We spent hours hanging over the side of their pens talking to our fellow shipmates and feeding them treats.

We arrived in Melbourne a week before the Royal party. Julie and I spent the interim becoming re-acquainted with Mike's parents, who made us very welcome and arranged several parties at their comfortable home with a beautiful garden. I was able to follow what Mike was doing by consulting the 'Blue Book' he had given me before we left, full title – *Itinerary and Outline of Programme of Commonwealth Tour 23 November 1953 – 15 March 1954. For Staff Use Only.*

The Blue Book told me, day by day and almost hour by hour, exactly where the Royal party was meant to be at any given moment. That was the essence of Mike's job as the Queen's and Prince Philip's combined travel agent and impresario – to get them to the right place at the right time with the right speech in their hands. Not to mention the two detectives, the secretaries, the accountant, the clerks, Bobo MacDonald, the pressmen, the doctors ... and a whole ship's crew.

It wasn't all work and no play. The Royal couple and their staff had seventeen days of relaxation on the voyage across the Pacific from Panama to the Fiji islands. When they crossed the equator, Prince Philip's detective presided as Neptune while Martin Charteris was Clerk of the Court, and Lady Alice Egerton and Lady Pamela Mountbatten (Ladies-in-Waiting) among the plaintiffs to receive interrogation and punishment. The Press Secretary, Richard Colville, revealed a humorous side to him rarely noticeable when he was on duty. He burlesqued Mae West as Queen Aphrodite with the words 'Come up and see me sometime' painted across his bare back.

* * *

In all the thousands of miles the Queen has travelled, in all the air and sea hours logged, one statistic – I would say the most important – cannot be calculated, namely, the effect of a royal visit on the emotions of the people visited. By now I had observed the reaction of British crowds to every conceivable royal occasion. Even so, when I arrived in Sydney to be reunited with Mike, I was stunned by the volume of public excitement that prevailed. It was just like

London during the Coronation, bursting at the seams with jostling, curious and noisy pedestrians.

Julie and I were berthed on a friend's yacht, the 'Ada', while Mike was booked into Government House for the duration of the stay. I would not be able to see him until he stepped ashore behind the Queen and Prince Philip. The *Gothic* was met out at sea by a small armada of ships and escorted into Sydney Harbour. The royal barge steered cautiously through a double line of yachts and ships (and surf boards) towards Farm Cove. As the barge drew level the excitement rose to such a pitch that I saw several people fall into the water from sheer exuberance. All the while sirens, hooters and whistles blared against the din of shouting and cheering. Every inch of dry land down to the waterline was dense with people.

The visit was long overdue, but doubly welcome for it. The Queen stepped ashore on the same spot as the first white settlers but to a welcome Australia had never seen before. The motorcade which followed was engulfed by the crowd. Mike confessed afterwards he found it frightening. Time and again along the route, the police cordon gave way under the pressure of people, slowing the Royal car to a snail's pace.

Today, when Popes and Presidents go walkabout regularly, such vast gatherings are not a rarity, but when the news reached London of the Royal car being impeded, there were murmurs of concern. Was the Queen safe? When I heard what some newspapers in England were writing, I felt ashamed. The Australian crowds were enthusiastic and warmhearted, informal without disrespect. But how could anybody know that who wasn't there?

Mike himself was accorded a hero's welcome on his return to his native land, local boy made good, extraordinarily so. From all over long-lost 'friends' appeared who wished to secure introductions to the Royal party. In vain! Mike was on duty practically twenty-four hours a day and the tour was so heavily planned in advance there was no room for anyone else.

The day after their arrival the Queen and Prince Philip began their intense schedule with the opening by the Queen of a session of the New South Wales Parliament. In her speech the Queen referred to the welcome of the day before – 'So spontaneous and cordial we shall always remember it ...'

In the soaring heat of the southern hemisphere summer, the fever of mass adulation soon became a strain. I remember one reception held in the restaurant on top of a large Sydney department store. Leaving late with the Royal party, Mike was leading the way through the haberdashery counters towards the exit after another long, hot, arduous day of meeting and greeting with another one already looming. Everybody in the party was feeling a bit jaded, too tired to think of anything but sleep. But Mike had a talent for relieving the situation when morale was sagging. Suddenly, he leapt over a counter and turned to the Queen obsequiously – 'Can I interest you in anything, Modom? I'm sure you'll find our selection quite adequate for your needs ...'

The Queen laughed the most. She was an accomplished mimic herself and on many occasions I've seen her give excellent impressions of the various VIPs she meets. She also does a very good Cockney.

Later, at a banquet at Government House in Sydney, it was my turn to raise a smile. I arrived to make the truly horrible discovery that I was the only woman wearing a tiara. As soon as the introductions were over, I slipped out of the room to hide it. At dinner, Prince Philip noticed it was missing and asked what had happened. He thought it was hilarious when I told him that, as I was searching for a safe hiding place, I'd heard voices approaching and ended up leaving my tiara beneath the nearest cushion and hoping for the best. Thankfully, after dinner I was able to retrieve it safely.

Although Sydney and Melbourne were the two main stops, the Royal tour also included Canberra, Hobart, Brisbane, Adelaide and Perth. As Julie and I wanted to be as near Mike as possible we did our best to follow the same route as the Royal party, with Mike arranging cars, planes and hotels along the way, although there were some days when it simply wasn't feasible to tag along. The Queen and Prince Philip flew across hundreds of miles of outback to reach some of the more inaccessible places; and some days they travelled by train.

I had entreated Mike to let me come to Australia

with one goal in mind – to salvage our marriage – but by agreeing to it he was breaking an iron rule in the Household, namely that wives do not accompany husbands on tours. Whenever I had suggested it previously, Mike's response had always been the same – 'You'll only clog up the works. It's the Royal show, no-one else's. Everything else has to be kept in the background.' I discovered that was certainly the way Prince Philip felt about wives on tour. Once, at the race track, he bumped into me accidentally as he turned to attract someone else's attention – 'What, you again,' he said. 'Everywhere we go you seem to turn up. You're getting like a piece of furniture around here.'

Before I could recover or apologise he had stalked off to join someone else. Mike overheard the remark and saw the tears welling up in my eyes – 'Don't upset yourself,' he said, in an attempt to console me. But I was upset.

For the duration of the Australian part of the tour – two whole months – Mike and I only had one night to ourselves, in Adelaide. We had dinner together and then went on to a nightclub but afterwards, Mike returned to Government House and I went back to my hotel, feeling empty. The evening had been enjoyable, of course but there had been no real connection, let alone the rekindling of love.

At no point, so far as I can remember, did Prince Philip attempt to intervene in the gradual deterioration of Mike's marriage, although he must have known about it. There was no attempt ever to lessen Mike's workload, nothing to contribute towards a reconciliation. In all fairness, perhaps it was Mike's own attitude that was largely to blame. He simply didn't want to work less. He wanted to work more. He loved his work, lived for it. The kind of life he had grown to enjoy would estrange him from me more and more, as many wives will understand.

Divorce seemed to be the inevitable solution. But with the Townsend affair still a highly sensitive issue, a divorce involving another member of the Royal Household would have been badly timed. Mike, I assumed, would prefer to maintain a semblance of outward normality until a more convenient moment. But what did he expect us to do in the in the meantime? Did he feel I should do the 'honourable thing' – have an affair to give *him* grounds for divorce? Questions like these dogged me on the long sea voyage back to London.

When Julie and I left for home, in a sister vessel of the *Wanstead*, I stood on deck watching until the last speck of land disappeared. Behind me the sun was setting in a flaming spectacle of colour which contrasted sharply with the sadness in my heart. I felt certain I would never see Australia again and it wasn't until that moment that I realised a chapter in my life was about to end.

The *S.S. Woodford* steamed back to England at a leisurely pace. She called at Colombo for a consignment of tea, and at Aden for fuel. Apart from these two stops there was nothing to interrupt the cycle of hot days followed by hot nights. Sometimes we didn't see another ship for days on end.

The Royal party had sailed in the *S.S. Gothic* ahead of us and when it reached Aden, they flew on to Tobruk, in Libya, where the Royal Yacht *Britannia* was waiting with Prince Charles and Princess Anne on board under the care of Boy Browning. After this family reunion, there was a brief visit to Malta to see Uncle Dickie and then on to Gibraltar. By this time we had also reached the Mediterranean and for the first time in weeks Mike was within radio-telephone range. We discussed the details of our arrival and, at the end of our conversation, Prince Charles asked Mike if he could speak to Julie. They carried on quite a long conversation, interspersed with fits of giggling and ending with an invitation from Prince Charles – 'See you at dancing, Julie.'

Despite the detour to Malta, *Britannia* made good time on the homeward passage for the official welcome at Tower Pier. It was a Royal return after an absence of six months and London turned out in force to welcome the Queen for the first time on *Britannia*. That night I attended the reception on board – almost out of breath as I had only just arrived myself.

Britannia's sleek outline was mirrored in fairy lights rippling across the Thames. It lifted my spirits to see so many familiar faces again. The Queen and Prince Philip looked tanned and relaxed. The arduous days crammed with innumerable crowds, the waving schoolchildren, the walkabouts, had not defeated them. The warmth of the home crowd's welcome merely reflected the success of the tour and for this success Mike was undoubtedly partly responsible. My pride in his achievement contrasted sadly with the failure of our own life together.

* * *

Chapter 17

Exit by Limelight

While I was in Australia I gathered from conversations within the Household that the romance between Princess Margaret and Peter Townsend was still running high in the news back home and that a majority of the public opinion was in favour of a marriage. Minority opinion included everybody in the Household. If Peter did marry Princess Margaret, the servant would become master and the thought of that was too shocking to contemplate.

The two principals in the drama were still being kept well apart, Peter Townsend in Brussels, his Princess in London. They kept in touch through letters and phone calls. But Peter was not weathering the storm particularly well. Already he had talked to the press and they had interpreted his comments to mean he was putting the weight of the decision on Princess Margaret's shoulders. She, meanwhile, had been given more royal duties in public and consequently more coverage in the newspapers and newsreels. To further divert her, with that all-important 25th birthday looming in August 1955, she was given a full Royal tour all of her own, one that would give her star billing in a series of exotic locations.

In January 1955, Princess Margaret and a modest suite of servants and two Ladies-in-Waiting flew off to the Caribbean to rendezvous with the Royal yacht *Britannia*. For the next five weeks, the Princess was filmed at banquets, receptions and motorcades right across the Caribbean. At night, in a succession of government mansions from Trinidad to Barbados, she glittered on the red carpet in tiara and long white gloves. By day, in open-topped limousines, looking stunning in her new wardrobe, she performed for the teams of reporters and camera-men who followed her every move.

The Caribbean trip brought Princess Margaret face-to-face with her Royal duty, and she seemed to enjoy it. Being a 'working' Princess certainly had its compensations. On the few occasions that Mike and I spoke on the subject, I gleaned the impression that Princess Margaret's attachment to Peter Townsend was beginning to waiver.

The final act was set for the Autumn of 1955. Princess Margaret celebrated her twenty-fifth birthday on August 21st, and the Press were poised for the announcement of an engagement on that day. When none was forthcoming, perplexed voices were raised. Was the whole affair over? Once more, the press looked to Townsend for the answer.

He was due in England on a month's leave during October.

I remember walking through Lowndes Square one afternoon soon after Peter Townsend's arrival. He was staying at the house of Lord Abergavenny. I was on the way to the bank. There was a crowd of reporters, photographers and bystanders around the door as Peter's car pulled up. He tried to jostle his way through but stumbled, and the pack closed in on him like hounds on a fox. The reporters actually held him back while the camera-men exploded flash bulbs in his face. It was pathetic to see him eventually wriggle free. The door opened a fraction and snapped shut the moment he had slipped through.

It was frightening to imagine how it might be for me in a similar situation. But I was in a similar situation. And it did turn out to be frightening.

Princess Margaret and Peter Townsend met for weekends in the country with mutual friends but they were hounded at every turn by journalists. Then, after the Queen returned from her holiday at Balmoral, a family conference was summoned. One night, Mike came home to change for dinner and said Princess Margaret and Peter Townsend had finally reached a decision – 'There's going to be an announcement tonight.'

'Which way has she gone?' I asked.

'The only way,' he replied.

Later in the evening a radio was brought in to the restaurant where we were dining. The BBC had interrupted their programme for a special news bulletin. Princess Margaret had issued a statement – 'I have decided not to marry Group Captain Peter Townsend. Mindful of the Church's teaching that Christian marriage is indissoluble, and conscious of the Commonwealth, I have resolved to put these considerations before any other … I am deeply grateful for the concern of all those who have constantly prayed for my happiness.'

With Princess Margaret and Peter Townsend reaching their ultimate decision, I guessed it would soon be time for Mike and me to do the same

* * *

As soon as possible after our return from Australia, I had gone up to Scotland to spend time with my parents and talk over the sad state of my marriage. By now, I was certain that Mike was having an affair. When I confronted him he told me to mind my own business. After pouring my heart out to my parents, they agreed that the only course open was a trial separation. It might bring Mike to his senses. Living in the same house, though sleeping apart, had become intolerable. And if my marriage was now none of my business whose was it? I took legal advice from a solicitor neighbour who told me to sit tight and leave it to Mike to make all the moves.

'Whatever happens,' Mike insisted, 'the Royal Family must be kept out of this.'

I entirely agreed with him. But I could hardly believe his next cynical suggestion.

'Of course, you'll have to be in the wrong,' he continued, 'My job comes first.'

I was devastated! More than any other thing, those few words spelled the end. For the sake of his career, and to protect the Royal Family from any unpleasantness, he wanted me to go against my conscience, shock my elderly parents, and perhaps alienate my children. I was horrified. My solicitor told me plainly that to be the guilty party in the divorce would reduce the possibility of my being awarded custody. That would have left Michael and Julie to the care of Mike, whose absences as a parent had contributed so much to the breakdown.

Throughout, Mike was confident that he could keep his job in the Household and that he would be able to arrange things accordingly. Certainly, I had no desire to see him forced into resigning. That would be a pointless sacrifice, considering that we both knew and accepted that our marriage was over. It would be ludicrous for Mike to lose both family and job, if it could possibly be avoided.

It was wretched to have to tell the children why their father was moving out of our home. I just couldn't find the words that would make sense to them and still be truthful. Mike left first to a friend's flat in Mayfair and then to a place of his own in Chelsea. We continued to keep in touch, mainly through lawyers, but also through his visits to Michael and

Julie. Being separated from them seemed to make Mike more aware of what he was about lose.

In the meantime, to preserve a sense of continuity at Launceston Place while the lawyers sorted out the divorce, the three of us tried to carry on as normally as possible while Mike concentrated on his duties at Buckingham Palace. The next overseas trip facing the Queen and Prince Philip was already being planned – to Nigeria.

To cheer us up, I gave a party for more than fifty children at the Hyde Park Hotel to celebrate Julie's seventh birthday. Both Prince Charles and Princess Anne were invited, together with Julie's school-mates and her palace dancing class friends. Her young guests were asked to arrive at 3.00 p.m. and the Royal children at 3.30, to allow me sufficient time to organise everything. Nurse Lightbody and one of the detectives arrived in a palace car on the stroke of 3.30 and when the chauffeur opened the door, two eager children shot up the steps. Upon seeing Julie Prince Charles rushed over to her – 'Hello, Julie, what a pretty dress, and where is the one with the butterfly on it?'

As well as ordering all the treats that young children love to eat, with Julie's favourite Ribena to quench their thirsts, I hired an entertainer to do conjuring tricks and lead the games. There was also dancing, naturally, though most of the boys seemed to prefer musical chairs and sliding about in their socks on the polished floor. Too soon the children who had all been so immaculate on arrival were looking distinctly disheveled.

When it was time to go home, both the Royal children thanked me so nicely that I felt a pang of regret that this might be my last time with them. In my position, facing divorce, a stigma had fallen on me. From now on, my visits to the palace were likely to be strictly about business, not for fun and friendship. For his part, Mike returned from the Nigerian tour to plunge straight into preparations for another one – Prince Philip was scheduled to open the 1956 Olympic Games in Melbourne and in due course Mike went to Australia to blaze the trail.

In April however, a family crisis brought us suddenly together again. My father had retired from the rope making business, and moved from Troon to a new home near Blairgowrie, in Perthshire. I was busy dealing with my solicitor in London, and decided to leave the children with their grand-parents for the Easter holidays.

Everything seemed to be going well, until the afternoon when Julie met the neighbouring farmer's children to play with some lambs in a nearby field surrounded by barbed wire. As Julie was saying goodbye to her friends, walking backwards, she turned and fell straight into the fence. The rusty wire tore part of the iris out of her left eye. The local doctor immediately drove her in his MG to Dundee Eye Infirmary, for emergency surgery.

When the grim news reached London, Mike arranged for both of us to fly up to Scotland and bring Julie back for expert treatment. However, by great good fortune, just as

Julie arrived at the hospital, Sir Stewart Duke-Elder, one of the leading eye surgeons in the country, was leaving the building. Sir Stewart was one of the Royal Family's consulting physicians and therefore knew who Mike Parker was. Recognising the seriousness of Julie's injury, he offered to operate straight away, a gesture that saved Julie's sight, for which we have ever been thankful.

* * *

As ex-Royal Navy officers, Prince Philip and Mike had shared more than a casual interest in the building of the royal yacht *Britannia* and, once all her sea trials were over, they were impatient to get their hands on her. So rather than go straight to the Melbourne Olympics and return by plane, Prince Philip decided to go part of the way on *Britannia*, with the justification that it would enable him to stop over at places otherwise considered too insignificant for a full Royal tour. In fact, by the time Prince Philip and Mike flew out to Mombasa in October 1956 to rendezvous with *Britannia*, they had a round-the-world voyage adventure ahead of them – via the Antarctic.

Accompanying them were a miscellaneous crew of naturalists and artists, among the latter, the painter Edward Seago. The 'funny friends' were afloat. When I saw Mike before his departure to discuss our own desperate problems, he was elated at the prospect of the trip ahead. It was going to be like the good old Navy days once more, no photographers, no wives, no children … freedom!

Soon afterwards, on the advice of my lawyer, I went to see the Buckingham Palace Press Secretary. Richard Colville. The time had come to think about the timing of a formal announcement of my separation from Mike. Richard Colville had handled Peter Townsend's divorce and the romance with Princess Margaret with tight-lipped disdain, but on the autumn afternoon when I went to see him, he showed me every consideration as well as sympathy. He understood fully the pressures Mike's work had put on our marriage. He also saw the personal differences that made a reconciliation virtually impossible. He regretted this, as a personal acquaintance of us both, but agreed that a separation and ensuing divorce seemed to be the only solution, and that the press would want to report it. His only request was that I delay any announcement until after Mike's return with Prince Philip from Melbourne. It is traditional for the City of London to hold a luncheon in the Guildhall to welcome Royalty after a prolonged absence abroad. This time, in addition, Prince Philip was scheduled to use the occasion to give a brief résumé of his world tour and Richard feared that a premature announcement from me might distract attention from Prince Philip's worthwhile achievements.

The children and I spent the New Year of 1957 with my mother and father in Scotland. Upon my return to London at the end of January, I instructed my lawyer to handle the whole matter discreetly and not to issue any statement until after the banquet at Guildhall. I respected Richard Colville too highly to want him to lose faith in me nor did I wish to hurt Prince Philip or Mike.

Having seen what the press had done to Peter Townsend I was under no illusions about how it would be for me and Mike. I was happy to wait for Mike to get back to London, so that I didn't have to face the expected storm of questions on my own. No one had anything to gain by not waiting. In the event, to my dismay, my lawyer prepared a statement in the appropriate style and released it without consulting me.

The Royal Yacht, *Britannia*, was sailing home the long way because of the 'Suez Crisis' which had seen British troops humiliated by a botched attempt to seize the waterway from Egyptian control. With the canal blocked by war damage, shipping from Australia had to sail to Europe by passing round the Cape and then heading north along the west African coat. *Britannia's* immediate destination was Gibraltar, which had been chosen as the rendezvous with the Queen who, after joining Prince Philip, would then lead a state visit to Portugal.

That was the moment my solicitor chose to make the announcement of my separation from Mike. I wasn't asked. I wasn't warned. And, to make matters worse, instead of releasing my statement through Reuters news agency my lawyer gave it as a scoop to the *Sunday Pictorial*.

When the news reached the *Britannia*, Mike was quick to cable a response to his solicitors, Messrs Summer and Company of Piccadilly – 'We are authorised to state that Lt. Cdr. Michael Parker has tendered his resignation as Private Secretary to the Duke of Edinburgh and that this has been accepted... The existing circumstances of his marriage make it impossible for him to carry on with his present occupation.'

On February 3rd the story was splashed on the front pages of nearly every British newspaper together with pictures of Prince Philip and Mike – 'Grim Duke sees off his Friend Parker' – 'Duke's Best Friend and Wife have Parted' – 'Parkers of the Palace Separate'. It was a ghastly re-run of the Princess Margaret – Peter Townsend affair, with newspapers asking their readers to take sides – me or Mike. People on the street were interviewed as to whether Mike should be allowed to stay in his job or not. I was in a state of shock. I could not understand why my solicitor's announcement, ill-timed though it was, should have upset all of Mike's plans to remain at Buckingham Palace.

Later on, I learned that both Prince Philip and the Queen had tried to dissuade Mike from resigning. Prince Philip had not only been Mike's employer but his closest friend. Time and again, the Queen had shown how much she appreciated Mike's support and loyalty. None of those most closely involved wanted Mike to quit, but that's what he did.

News reporters and photographers pestered me on the phone for a comment and loitered outside the house. They

253

harassed the nanny. They intercepted Julie on her way home from school. When I tried to smuggle her to safety with a nearby friend, the reporters followed us. When I popped out to the grocer's, they came into the shop to bombard me with questions.

Some newspapers, to be fair to the press overall, were able to see things from my point of view – 'Are we being unfair to women like Mrs. Parker?' asked *The Sunday Express*. 'Are we being fair to these men who help to run our modern monarchy? Are we not placing an almost unbearable strain on them and on their wives and children at home?... Townsend was the first of the democratic courtiers. And his wife, in her little house in Windsor Great Park, was the first of the modern royalty widows, the first of those women who wait alone while their husbands shine... It is a miracle that marriage on these terms actually survives...'

Such forthright opinions inevitably brought a response from Buckingham Palace, which once again found itself facing the charge of home-wrecking. At some point, *The Sunday Mirror* must have received a phone call from Richard Colville – 'It has been suggested that royal tours and holidays are keeping husbands and wives apart to such an extent that the situation could even lead to a breakdown of marriage... I am authorised to state that such allegations are completely untrue...'

For weeks after the first sensational headlines I received poison-pen letters accusing me of timing the news of our separation to be vindictive. Only my real friends realised what I had been going through and understood the whole story.

Mike was present at the luncheon in the Guildhall when Prince Philip presented a summary of his world tour. He was seated as near as possible without actually being at Prince Philip's side. The gesture was not overlooked. But Prince Philip only made the vaguest reference in his speech to the unhappy publicity surrounding his return – 'I believe there are things for which it is worthwhile making some personal sacrifice, and I believe that the British Commonwealth is one of these things.'

Later that month, Mike received a token of esteem from the Queen who invested him with the insignia of a Commander of the Royal Victorian Order.

* * *

On October 5th 1957, I filed the petition for divorce. The key witness in the case was Mike's cook and part-time housekeeper, Mrs. Kyra Semi, a former opera singer who performed under the stage name Kyra Vance. The co-respondent was named as Mrs Mary Alexandra Thompson, whose true identity was never revealed.

On February 28th 1958, I was granted my divorce from Lieutenant-Commander Michael Parker, CVO, RN. in a brief formal hearing. It took fifteen minutes to wind up a marriage of fifteen years. The case was uncontested. Mike was in Mexico at the time and Mrs Thompson did not come forward. I was given custody of our two children and Mike was granted reasonable access.

Mike continued to make the headlines for years. He was romantically linked to various glamorous women. He still counted Prince Philip as a personal friend, and they continued to meet socially as in the old days.

As the children grew up, Mike kept in touch with them. It is all too easy for a hostility to sour a divorce but I went out of my way to make sure this could not happen.

I last saw Mike in June of 1972 at Julie's wedding. He had flown over from Australia to be by Julie's side and give her away. Prince Philip was also there as her godfather. He and I exchanged inconsequential remarks about the traffic and the weather. For one flickering moment, I seemed to see once more how it had all begun – with Prince Philip and his bride watching Mike and me start off the dance, at a different wedding, in a different world, a lifetime ago.

We turned aside to mingle with the other guests. The door to the past was closed.

* * *

Made in the USA
San Bernardino, CA
17 January 2018